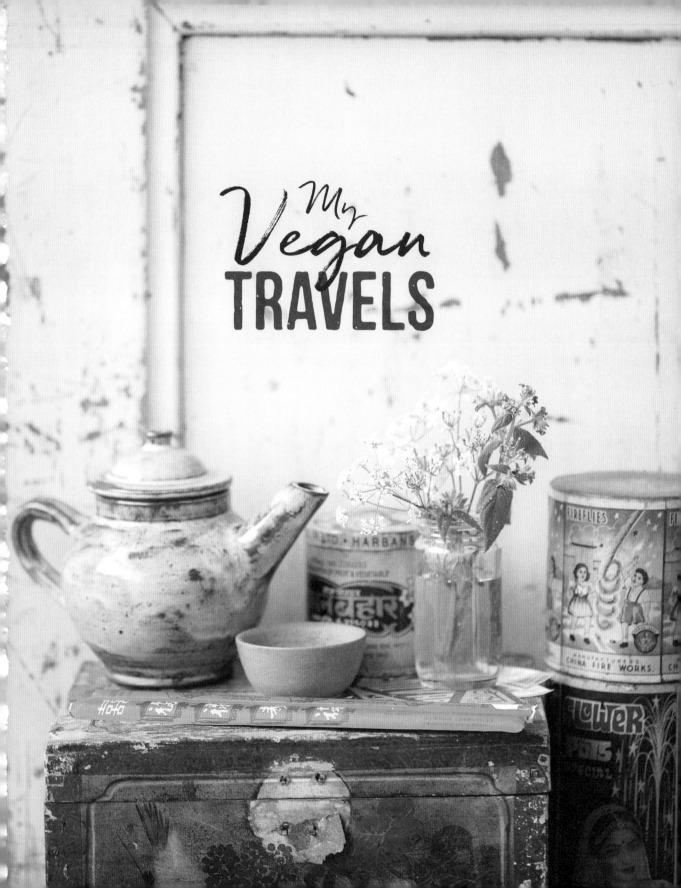

My Vegan TRAVELS

COMFORT FOOD INSPIRED BY ADVENTURE

JACKIE KEARNEY
PHOTOGRAPHY BY CLARE WINFIELD

rps

RYLAND PETERS & SMALL
LONDON • NEW YORK

Senior Designer Megan Smith
Editor Kate Reeves-Brown
Production Controller Mai-Ling Collyer
Art Director Leslie Harrington
Picture Research Christina Borsi
Editorial Director Julia Charles
Publisher Cindy Richards

Food Stylists Emily Kydd and Jackie Kearney
Prop Stylist Tony Hutchinson
Indexer Hilary Bird

Published in 2017 by
Ryland Peters & Small
20–21 Jockey's Fields
London WC1R 4BW
and
341 East 116th Street
New York, NY 10029

www.rylandpeters.com

10 9 8 7 6 5 4 3 2 1

Text © Jackie Kearney 2017

Design and commissioned
photography © Ryland
Peters & Small 2017

ISBN 978-1-84975-883-3

A CIP record for this
book is available from the
British Library. US Library
of Congress CIP data has
been applied for.

Printed in China

Notes
• Both British (Metric) and
American (Imperial plus US
cups) measurements are
included in these recipes
for your convenience,
however it is important
to work with one set of
measurements and not
alternate between the
two within a recipe.
• All spoon measurements
are level unless otherwise
specified.
• Ovens should be
preheated to the
specified temperatures.
We recommend using an
oven thermometer. If using
a fan-assisted oven, adjust
temperatures according
to the manufacturer's
instructions.
• When a recipe calls for
the grated zest of citrus
fruit, buy unwaxed fruit
and wash well before using.
If you can only find treated
fruit, scrub well in warm
soapy water before using.

CONTENTS

INTRODUCTION 6

MY VEGAN JOURNEY 8

MY VEGAN STORE CUPBOARD 10

A FEW BASIC RECIPES 12

No place
LIKE HOME 18

European
SUMMERS 60

Asian
COMFORT 100

AMERICANA 158

INDEX 204

ACKNOWLEDGEMENTS 208

INTRODUCTION

YOU CAN TAKE THE GIRL OUT OF MANCHESTER BUT …

I challenge you to find a northerner who doesn't love their comfort food. I think we all do. But for those of us whose homes (and hearts) are nestled along the Pennine backbone of the UK and beyond, we truly love, or should that be need, our comfort food to warm us through from all that rain and wind. I think that's why we love pies so much. In one Lancashire town, famous for their love of pies, the Wigan 'kebab' serves a meat and potato pie inside a bread roll known as a barmcake. Perhaps there's an inevitable link between comfort food and Northerners.

Comfort food is more than just fuel to our hard-working bodies, it makes us feel comforted from the inside out, and of course satisfies the biggest of appetites. I'm one of these hungry ones. Don't be misled by my love of noodle soups and stir-fries. Since I first became a vegetarian in my mid teens, I've spent decades recreating the home-cooked food of my northern childhood. Eating out was never great for a vegetarian back then, but there were no limits to what the home cook could change and adapt in their own kitchen.

I wanted to write about comfort food because I knew it was a way to bring together all the comfort-style recipes that I have loved from my childhood and travels, and have seen my own children enjoy. I decided to write about what comfort food means to me, before I read someone else's description. And I thought it was a lot about memories. And home. And feeling warm and satisfied. It can also be about dishes that remind us of places where we felt happy, nurtured and sated, any or all of these things. Remember the times when you were poorly as a child and the dish that made you feel a little better (tomato soup, in my case). Or visiting your relatives for a big family dinner and for me, looking forward to Aunty Pat's apple pie. Or dad's moules marinière (French-style mussels), because it's the only thing he seemed to cook for a while after he and mum separated (and we all pretended we loved it as much as he did). Or the dishes that whisk you back to that place or moment in time that felt so perfect. For me, that is eating noodle soup with my family by the Mekong (you had that recipe already, Siam soup in *Vegan Street Food*) or a simple lunch with my husband Lee in my favourite thali café in Manchester.

You will find many street food recipes amongst these pages, because street food is so evocative of places and times, and these memories often bring back those feelings of happiness and satisfaction. And because street food is probably my heartsong[1] when it comes to food. Or is it because of the wonderful memories this food evokes, and that it's travel that's really my true heartsong? The fact that I travel with a lightweight mountain stove in my backpack perhaps answers that question. While in a small village in Northern Thailand, I once cooked mashed potato and vegan sausages (from a packet of dried sosmix I was also carrying) on my little stove to help the kids feel more at home. Good comfort food does make us feel at home. In truth, I've made mashed potatoes for the children on more than one occasion while we've been travelling, including on a beach on a remote Indonesian island and at a friend's house in Kathmandu. Suffice it to say my Nepalese buddy was so overwhelmed with the comforting hug that comes from a good mash, he still talks about it to this day.

[1] *Happy Feet* (the movie) depicts penguins who sing. Each penguin discovers that they have a unique song that vocalizes what is already in their heart; their heartsong. I think this applies to many things that humans do when we create something from a passion.

Clockwise from top left: British Colombia, Canada; fruit seller, Italy; sunset in downtown LA; Portland hipster van, Oregon; Langtang Valley stupa, Nepal; Basket seller, Cambodia.

MY VEGAN JOURNEY

I think vegetarian comfort food is easier to achieve in some ways, as cheese must be one of the most used ingredients in such recipes. It's one of the reasons I became more interested in vegan food, despite being vegetarian. It's just all too much cheese for my liking at times (and my well-being, and the cows' well-being, and the planet, to be fair). Developing vegan comfort recipes has been a long and slow burner in my kitchen, a bit like some of the food.

With many comfort food recipes I read about, I find myself tempted by the ideas but often left hungry, because meat or fish are the central component. As I've said before, it's not as straightforward as replacing the meat with a plant-based substitute (although there are some dishes where this works well, such as a sauce-based curry). This is often because the flavour of the dish comes from the meat itself, or often the bones. Meat substitutes are good for reproducing texture in a dish, but they rarely bring flavour to the party. And without any additional preparation, they can sometimes taste a little off-putting, such as canned gluten (or seitan), textured vegetable protein (TVP, usually made from soya/soy) or fresh tofu or tempeh. But with a few little tricks and additional ingredients, these can also help vegan food taste more substantial, as well as providing those essential plant-based proteins.

I have been incredibly lucky to explore and sample so many vegan and vegetarian dishes throughout my travels, and this has given me the inspiration to develop lots of other recipes, not just from the exotic street corners of Asia, but from my own childhood and more recent travel adventures with my now teenage children.

ON THE ROAD AGAIN

As a family, we have returned to Asia twice since our 'gap year' together in 2005. Prior to the children starting high school, which always felt like it signalled the end of our extended trips together, we took them out of school several months before the end of their final year in primary school. We started our trip by getting married in Kandy in Sri Lanka, as we had promised to the children. And then we set off on another adventure, taking in places we had to omit on the previous trip. We spent four glorious months in Nepal and returned to Indonesia to continue our journey across my favourite archipelago. This still remains firmly on my future travel agenda as I have yet to reach the Maluku islands.

After I dragged them around South East Asia yet again a few years ago, they made me promise that they could choose the next trip. And like many British teenagers, they are fascinated with America. It was a big year for us as a family, with them leaving home for university. So I wanted to grab the opportunity for some travel time together while I could still convince them to come with us. I'm glad we let them direct us this time, because it's led us to places and experiences I might not have chosen.

I have to be honest here. I was very sceptical about American food. But North America really took me by surprise with food in general, and indeed with the whole vegan thing. Some of the produce is extraordinary, and I was blown away by the quality in places. The food culture is incredibly vibrant and the nature of fusion in food went beyond my normal dining experiences. It was bold and confident, and sometimes downright amusing (Japanese fusion hotdogs anyone?). But it was the attitudes towards vegan foods that really stopped me in my tracks.

While vegan food in Asia is just part of the landscape, and what many people eat because it's accessible and affordable, it felt like a completely different creature in North America. It's gentrified to some extent, especially in LA and New York. But there are so many opportunities to eat really good vegan food. And not once did we feel like a nuisance, as vegans and vegetarians so often do in some restaurants. It's much more part of the mainstream food landscape than in Europe, with dedicated vegan menus and wide-ranging choices that were often skilfully made and simply delicious. Instead of getting lost in chaotic outdoor markets in Asia, I would get lost for hours in supermarkets in America. And I mean hours. We turned road trip and hotel picnics into a new art form.

The trip took shape in early 2016. I told the publisher about my idea for a new book, and that whilst most of it was already drafted in some form or another, I was going to do some more research in North America. Although my work is adaptable to lengthier trips, my husband's is less so. So we planned a trip where I would travel solo for a month and then my family would join me. The opportunity of two months of travel led to some rather outrageous travel plans. Having no real sense of the vast size of North America, I have always been fascinated with the coastal journey from the southern tip of California, all the way to Alaska, and made a mental note many years ago that one day I would make this journey. I love travelling overland because it connects you more to the people you meet. But there is no doubt it's a much slower way to go. When the children decided they wanted to travel across the southern states of America, it made a natural loop. LA became their arrival point, so I decided to look for a northern starting point for my section of the journey and my

friend Maya's place in Vancouver seemed like a very good place to start.

We met Maya in a sweltering Gokarna station in Karnataka, South India. As a lone Canadian woman travelling across India, Maya has taught me so much about how to travel well. She taught us how to read the stars at night, how to cope with long Indian train journeys (imported red wine) and that dosas can be eaten for breakfast, lunch and dinner if that's what makes you happy. The fact that we both adore food and cooking has meant our long-distance bond has weathered the years. Maya leapt at the chance to join me in America, and we spent a month together travelling down the North West Pacific Coast, from Vancouver via Oregon and down through California, before meeting up with the rest of my family for a summer road trip across America. Just like the old days in India, but with flushing toilets.

This book brings together delicious and comforting vegan recipes inspired by dishes from around the globe. From British and European comfort classics to fusion and street food-inspired dishes from Asia and North America, each one satisfies the soul as well as the appetite. As the sign above my street kitchen used to say: 'Inspired by World Food. Made In Manchester.'

'I'm a Northern girl, wild and free
I've got four strong winds to carry me
I've been East to West and all around the world
But I'll always be a Northern girl
Where I come from
What I'm made of
Where I wanna be
You can take me out of there
But you can't take it out of me.'

MY VEGAN STORE CUPBOARD

PLANT-BASED PROTEIN

In my experience, most vegan substitutes for meat are purely about bringing texture to a dish. Rarely will vegetable protein have any intrinsic flavour, such as gluten or soya. But that doesn't stop me using them as they provide easy access to some essential protein. What's important for me here, is about eating a variety of nutritious foods and creating robust and intense flavours at the same time. The first cook to get me thinking about this was actually Linda McCartney. My mum bought me a copy of her very first cookbook back in the mid-80s, and I found myself seeking out textured vegetable proteins (TVP) on the shelves of my local health food shop.

There is a huge debate about meat-like food made from plant-based proteins, with people arguing against the use of the same terminology (with arguments about artisan skills and the original meanings in our language). There has even been a backlash to all this, with supermarket giant Sainsbury's renaming their vegan 'cheese' Gary.

I'm a firm believer that language changes and adapts over time, and personally have no issue with calling a veggie burger, well, a burger. Or even having vegan 'charcuterie'. Of course I know it's not charcuterie, which is an artisan skill of preserving meat. But it helps me locate (within my cooking) where I might eat that product as a so-called substitute, such as vegan 'pepperoni' on my pizza.

I like making seitan from time to time, and it's a useful texture that makes a healthy change from soy-based proteins, especially if you use vital wheat gluten to make your own. I love the work of Sgaia who sell small-batch vegan 'butchery'/'charcuterie' in the UK. In the US, there has been a proliferation of these well-made plant-based products (Oregon being a particular hotspot for production). It was great to see and experience, and I filled half a suitcase with the vegan produce I gathered over two months. Some were revolting. But some were astounding. And I think it's important not to throw the baby out with the bathwater.

VEGAN SUBSTITUTES FOR DAIRY

This is one of the most challenging areas of vegan cooking. It's very difficult for an old-school vegetarian like myself to face a food future with no cheese. But after watching Cowspiracy I made a commitment to myself to work towards a fully vegan diet by eating vegan food for five days each week; a 5:2 vegan so to speak. Everybody is different and some people have better access to alternatives than others, but some of the key ingredients for making savoury sauces and cheesy flavoured alternatives can easily be found online. I was nervous when I first starting cooking with them, but then I remembered my early forays into cooking with tofu (soggy and tasteless) and decided it was worth sticking with it. Following my West Coast USA trip, I have become more confident with some of these products. Nutritional yeast is not a product to be feared!

Most major supermarkets produce a variety of vegan 'dairy' products including 'cheeses' and 'yogurts'. My favourite vegan cheese is made by Violife, who have launched American-style slices as well as an excellent vegan 'Parmesan' and 'mozzarella' in the UK. I wouldn't eat them on their own. But they are great for cooking with. It's possible to buy some excellent plant-based milks, yogurts, butters and creams now (from Alpro, The Coconut Collaborative, Koko and Oatly among others) and there is now a wide variety beyond just soy-based. For egg substitutes, I prefer to grind linseeds/flaxseeds into a paste or use silken tofu. Gram flour also makes a good protein-based binding agent. I also make my own cashew cream, almond milk and almond 'ricotta'.

A FEW BASIC RECIPES

CASHEW CREAM

Making your own vegan cream is as easy as buying a carton from the shop, and the nutritional value will be far greater. To save on costs, buy unsalted raw cashews in large bags from an Indian grocer. The cream will keep for 5 days in the fridge.

140 g/scant 1¼ cups raw cashews
350 ml/1½ cups filtered water, plus extra for soaking
½ teaspoon salt

MAKES 500 ML/2 CUPS

Soak the raw cashews in filtered water for 2–3 hours. Drain and rinse. Add the rinsed nuts to the filtered water and salt, and blitz in a food processor or blender until completely smooth. Add more water to achieve the required consistency.

ALMOND MILK

Like cashew cream, almond milk is better when homemade. If the almonds are unskinned (brown), you will need to soak them for an hour or so in warm water, and remove the skins by rubbing with your fingers before soaking again and blending. Store in the fridge for 5 days.

260 g/2 cups raw blanched almonds
500 ml/2 cups filtered water, plus extra for soaking

MAKES 750 ML/3 CUPS

Soak the almonds in filtered water overnight. Drain and rinse, then blend until smooth with the filtered water. Pour the mixture through muslin/cheesecloth. The milky liquid can be diluted with water to reach the required consistency, and the almond residue can be kept and chilled as 'ricotta' (see page 15). You can also add flavours to it or even leave it to ferment.

EASY VEGAN MAYONNAISE

Aquafaba, or chickpea water, has been a revelation for me over the last year or two. Basically the water in that can of chickpeas has enough protein in it that it can be wildly transformed. Making macarons is a step too far for me, and it's not that stable as meringue, but aquafaba mayo is very easy to make and much more cost-effective than the expensive shop-bought stuff.

2 small garlic cloves, crushed
1 tablespoon lemon juice
2 teaspoons Dijon mustard
3 tablespoons liquid from a can
   of chickpeas, plus 12 whole chickpeas
120 ml/½ cup vegetable oil
60 ml/¼ cup extra virgin olive oil
½ teaspoon salt
½ teaspoon black pepper

MAKES 250 ML/1 CUP

Using a food processor or stick blender, blitz the garlic, lemon juice, mustard, chickpea liquid and chickpeas until completely smooth. With the blender running, slowly add the vegetable oil until the mixture becomes smooth and creamy.

Transfer to a bowl, and whisk constantly while slowly pouring in the olive oil. Season with salt and pepper. Transfer to clean jar or container. The mayo will keep for a week in the fridge.

ALMOND 'RICOTTA' AND CREAM

This vegan substitute for ricotta is a versatile ingredient, and delicious with salads. Try it with sweet tomatoes and watermelon for a deliciously simple starter. It will keep in the fridge for 5 days.

260 g/2 cups raw blanched almonds, soaked
    in filtered water overnight, drained and rinsed
250 ml/1 cup filtered water
1/3 teaspoon acidophilus (optional)

MAKES 500 G/2 CUPS

Blend the drained almonds with the water and acidophilus, if using, until smooth. Place in muslin/cheesecloth, twist and leave overnight in the fridge to drain. The liquid can be used as almond cream.

MINTED 'RICOTTA'

Herbed ricotta is at its best when eaten within a day or two. You can experiment with your favourite herbs' tender leaves like basil, chives and coriander/cilantro. You can also add other flavours such as black pepper or chilli/hot pepper flakes.

260 g/2 cups raw blanched almonds, soaked
    in filtered water overnight, drained and rinsed
250 ml/1 cup filtered water
1/3 teaspoon acidophilus (optional)
6 g/1/4 cup freshly chopped mint
1 small garlic clove, finely minced
1 teaspoon salt
1/2 teaspoon black pepper
2 teaspoons freshly squeezed lemon juice

MAKES 500 G/2 CUPS

Blend the drained almonds with the water and acidophilus, if using, until smooth. Place in muslin/cheesecloth, twist and leave overnight in the fridge to drain. Add the remaining ingredients, mix well and leave to set in the fridge for a few hours.

FLAX 'EGG'

There are a number of techniques for making egg replacements in vegan cooking. Chickpea water used to make aquafaba is also very popular, but I find it can be rather inconsistent for baking.

My personal favourite is the flax 'egg'. For a start, it's highly nutritious as it uses ground linseeds/flaxseeds which are full of essential omega-3 and omega-6 fatty acids. I use plain linseeds/flaxseeds, but you can use the hulled version if you prefer. It makes little difference, other than cost, as the seeds are ground to a paste anyway.

You will need a spice or coffee grinder, or the ubiquitous Nutribullet. A good grinder is an essential piece of equipment for grinding any seeds to a consistent powder. Flax 'eggs' will keep for up to 3 days in the fridge. You may find you need to add more water to the mixture after a day or two, as it tends to thicken further as time goes on.

1 tablespoon freshly ground linseeds/flaxseeds
3 tablespoons filtered water

MAKES 1 EGG REPLACER

To make one egg, mix together the freshly ground linseeds/flaxseeds and water. Place in the fridge for about 20–30 minutes and the mixture will become gel-like and ready to use as an egg substitute. To save time, I make four or five times this quantity as it will keep in the fridge for a few days. You can also substitute chia seeds if you like.

VEGAN PASTRY

This pastry is based on Michel Roux's pâte brisée, a deliciously short and crumbly pastry that he recommends for flans and pies. I have experimented with numerous vegan substitutions for his pastry recipes, and I find that silken tofu makes a great egg replacement. Silken tofu has a fantastic texture for making dough or even vegan quiche. You will find it in the fridge at any Japanese or Chinese supermarket, and it has a long shelf-life.

150 g/5 oz. vegan 'margarine' such
   as Stork (or coconut butter)
250 g/scant 2 cups plain/all-purpose
   flour, plus extra for dusting
pinch of caster/superfine sugar
1 teaspoon salt
1 tablespoon almond milk, plus extra
   for brushing
50 g/2 oz. silken tofu

MAKES 450 G/1 LB.

To prepare the pastry, rub the margarine, flour, sugar and salt together to make a rough crumb, then add the milk and tofu to form a soft dough. Knead gently so well combined, then wrap in clingfilm/plastic wrap and place in the fridge for 20 minutes.

ROASTED VEGETABLE STOCK

This roasted stock will bring an intense and robust flavour to lots of recipes, especially soups and stews. It will keep in the fridge for a week or it can be frozen.

1 celery bunch, roughly chopped
2 large fennel bulbs, roughly chopped
8 carrots, peeled and thickly sliced
3 onions, skin on, quartered
2 beef/beefsteak tomatoes, quartered
3 tablespoons olive oil
480 ml/2 cups red wine, such as Syrah
5 litres/5¼ quarts water
400-g/14-oz. can cannellini or white
   beans, rinsed
2 bay leaves
2-cm/¾-inch sprig of tender rosemary
30 g/1 oz. dried porcini mushrooms
   or other dried mushrooms
1 teaspoon peppercorns
1 teaspoon salt

MAKES 2 LITRES/QUARTS

Preheat the oven to 190°C (375°F) Gas 5. Lay the celery, fennel, carrots, onions and tomatoes on a baking sheet. Drizzle with the olive oil and place in the preheated oven for 45 minutes until the vegetables are well charred and very soft.

Transfer the vegetables to a large stock pot. Then place the empty roasting pan over medium heat and add the wine. Scrape up all the crispy and blackened bits from the bottom and then pour the contents into the stock pot.

Add the water, beans, herbs, dried mushrooms, peppercorns and salt to the pan and place over high heat. Bring to the boil and simmer for 1½–2 hours. The stock should be reduced to less than half the original quantity. Remove from the heat and strain the reduced stock through a fine sieve/strainer. Set aside to cool.

MISO GRAVY

This versatile gravy is packed with umami, the deep savoury taste often found in meat-based gravy. The sauce makes a great accompaniment to a traditional vegan roast dinner such as savoy-wrapped quinoa roast (see page 42) or with my big fat veggie cottage pie (see page 45). It can also be simply poured over roasted vegetables. The gravy will keep for 3–4 days in the fridge and can be reheated as needed.

60 ml/4 tablespoons olive oil or
   60 g/2 oz. vegan margarine
1 tablespoon plain/all-purpose flour
1 litre/4¼ cups roasted vegetable stock
   (see opposite)
1 tablespoon miso or soy bean paste
½–1 teaspoon salt, to taste

MAKES 1 LITRE/QUART

Heat the oil or margarine in a medium pan or frying pan/skillet, then add the flour and mix together to make a paste.

Cook gently over low-medium heat for about 1–2 minutes, then start adding the vegetable stock a little at a time. Mix well to ensure all the lumps have dissolved. Keep adding the stock (using a whisk can be easier at this stage). Bring to a simmer, mixing well to ensure a smooth, thick gravy.

Add the miso or soy bean paste and salt and stir well. Taste the gravy and add a little more salt if needed.

CHILLI PICKLE

Mrs G's chilli and crab apple pickle is super simple to prepare, and brings a tangy, spicy punch on the side for lots of subcontinent snacks, dals and curries. The pickle will keep for several weeks in a sterilized jar in the fridge.

20 small green finger chillies/chiles
2 crab apples
1 teaspoon black mustard seeds
½ teaspoon salt
120 ml/½ cup freshly squeezed lemon juice
½ teaspoon ground turmeric

MAKES 250 G/9 OZ.

To make the pickle, cut off the top of the chillies/chiles and slice them lengthways. Place in a small bowl. Slice the crab apples in half, remove the cores, then cut each half into 2-mm/1/16-inch slices.

Grind the mustard seeds a little using a pestle and mortar. Add the salt, lemon juice and ground turmeric. Mix well and add to the chillies/chiles and apple. Mix well and place in a sterilized jar. Leave for a few days in the fridge until the lemon juice has 'cooked' the mixture slightly.

No place LIKE HOME

CHILDHOOD MEMORIES AND HOME-COOKED COMFORTS

NO PLACE LIKE HOME

There are numerous cooks and chefs who inspire my cooking at home and make me very hungry with their passionate approach to food. With chefs like Ottolenghi, my absolute food hero, the words imaginative, bold and flavourful spring to mind. I don't mind the sometimes long shopping lists, because I know it can take a little bit of effort to make plant-based dishes with this kind of depth and complexity.

Then there are chefs, or rather cooks, who occupy that place in my foodie heart that is warm and cosy, and make me feel nurtured and comforted. I've been a fan of Nigel Slater's food for a very long time. I love his gentle approach to slowed-down cooking and combining simple store cupboard ingredients with perfect seasonal produce. He makes food that you could imagine lighting you up after a long day at work and stumbling through a windy front door to a warm house and the waft of delicious aromas. This is how I imagine Nigel's house. And I always wanted to create that home. Somewhere safe, warm and nurturing. I guess this has shaped my approach in the kitchen as cooking itself has always made me feel comforted (perhaps less so in the hectic MasterChef kitchen or at a busy festival with my street food kitchen). But I also love to create those feelings of warmth and nurture at home for my own children and family. I hope it's what will bring my children home sometimes, as they move on in the world.

Most of the recipes in this section have been created in my home kitchen, cooking for my family. I love nothing more than having my mum, sisters and their families joining us around our big family dining

From left to right: Castlefield Canal; view of Beetham Tower from Rochdale Canal; Manchester China Town; The Rainy City; view over Manchester from the Derbyshire hills; a colourful display at a West Indian Grocer.

table and tucking into Sunday dinner, a long-standing British tradition. This section includes recipes from the numerous feasts I have cooked over the years, where the reliance of the big family dinner has not been the roasted joint of meat, but vegetables instead. Following my first (and only) disappointing vegetarian Christmas dinner at a relative's house, my kitchen endeavours for the family roast dinner centred on making sure that the vegetable dishes never sit sadly in the corner. Many of these dishes have become big favourites with meat-eating family and friends too. It's all part of my sneaky plan to adapt their eating habits by stealth with tasty food.

You may notice there are few salads sitting amongst the recipes in this section. If you are familiar with our northern UK climate and rainfall, you will know there is a very good reason why this is so.

Manchester has about one-third less sunshine than London, and what Londoners call 'windy', we call a good drying day. That's the reason our meal times at home are dominated by warming dishes. There's a time and place for salad, and a cold, rainy Manchester afternoon is generally not one of them.

You will also notice that there are dishes in this section that don't seem very traditionally British. I like to use local ingredients as much as I can, but I do have a dry store cupboard packed with spices from around the globe, and this often leads to more fusion-style recipes. The dishes here simply reflect the warming comfort and family meals that I make in my own home, which sometimes draw on flavours from my own childhood or local influences that have made their mark on dining tables in British homes, such as West Indian or Polish food.

ROASTED TOMATO SOUP
with paprika tortilla straws

Tomato soup is a British comfort food classic. For me, and now my own children, it represents childhood comfort food. It is what mum used to make me when I needed looking after. Of course, there are other variations, but for many people, only the one that comes out of the famous red can will ever be good enough. When I was 10 years old, I went for lunch at my friend Lindsey's house, and her mum topped our tomato soup with big homemade crusty croutons and grated cheese. I was suitably impressed, having never had homemade croutons or soup toppings before. Now I can't eat soup without piling something on the top. This is a great way to make use of plentiful ripe tomatoes.

TO MAKE THE SOUP
2 kg/4½ lb. fresh ripe tomatoes
3 small red onions, quartered
6 whole garlic cloves, skins on
1 tablespoon vegetable oil
1.5 litres/6¼ cups vegetable stock
1–2 teaspoons salt, to taste
1 teaspoon white pepper

TO MAKE THE PAPRIKA TORTILLA STRAWS
2 flour tortillas
1 tablespoon freshly chopped thyme
1 tablespoon mild paprika powder
1 teaspoon salt
pinch of chilli/chili powder (optional)
60 ml/¼ cup pomace oil

TO MAKE THE BASIL OIL
handful of basil leaves
200 ml/scant 1 cup extra virgin olive oil
½ teaspoon salt

TO SERVE
vegan cream (optional)

2 large baking sheets, very lightly oiled

SERVES 4

Preheat the oven to 200°C (400°F) Gas 6.

Using a small, sharp paring knife, remove the top part of the hard core from each of the tomatoes. Place the tomatoes on one of the prepared baking sheets, tops facing up. On the second baking sheet, lay the onion quarters and garlic cloves and drizzle with the oil. Place both baking sheets in the oven and roast for 40 minutes. Remove the onions and garlic cloves, but continue to cook the tomatoes for a further 20 minutes until completely softened and sticky. Set aside to cool.

Reduce the oven to 140°C (280°F) Gas 1 for the paprika straws.

To make the paprika straws, using a large, sharp knife, slice the tortillas into quarters, then slice them into strips, 3–4 mm/⅛ inch wide. In a large bowl, place the thyme, paprika, salt and chilli/chili powder, if using. Add the tortilla strips and toss until well covered. Drizzle with the oil and toss again until well coated.

Lay the tortilla strips on a baking sheet and bake in the low oven for 20 minutes until golden brown and crispy. Remove from the oven and transfer to paper towels to cool and drain any excess oil.

Meanwhile, using your hands, squeeze out the garlic from the cloves and discard the skins. Then remove and discard the skins from the tomatoes (leave the skins on if you prefer or want to save time). Tip the onions, garlic and tomatoes into a large, deep pan and add the stock. Using a hand blender, purée the soup until smooth. Bring to the boil, then simmer over low heat for 10 minutes. Add salt and pepper to taste.

To make the basil oil, combine the fresh basil with the extra virgin olive oil and salt. Using a food processor or blender, blitz until completely smooth. This will keep for several weeks in a clean bottle in the fridge.

Serve the warm soup in big bowls, with a pile of crispy tortilla straws on top and drizzled with basil oil and vegan cream, if using.

TEMPEH 'BACON', LETTUCE AND TOMATO SANDWICH
with gochujang mayonnaise

How on earth do you live without bacon? Definitely one of the top five questions that vegans and veggies get asked. Who says vegan food can't get down and dirty with the big boys? This vegan take on the classic BLT is everything you could want from a sandwich. And it's unbelievably delicious! I dare you to try it. Just once. You'll be coming back for more, I promise you. Tempeh is simply soy beans, fermented and compressed. You can buy tempeh, plain or smoked, from wholefood shops, South East Asian grocery stores and online suppliers. Unlike tofu, it contains the whole soy bean, so tempeh has much higher protein, vitamin and fibre contents, as well as more 'bite' in its texture. Tempeh also tends to be less processed than tofu and it is much easier to source from non-GM organic soy beans.

160 g/5½ oz. smoked tempeh, sliced lengthways into 5 mm/¼ inch thick slices
125 ml/½ cup tamari or light soy sauce
2 tablespoons vegan mayonnaise (see page 12)
½ tablespoon gochujang (Korean red pepper paste)
1 tablespoon pomace or vegetable oil
2 thick slices of your favourite bread, lightly toasted
handful of iceberg lettuce, sliced
handful of watercress or lamb's lettuce
1 large ripe tomato, sliced
pickled chillies/chiles (optional)

SERVES 1

Marinate the tempeh slices in the tamari or light soy sauce for 10 minutes.

Mix together the vegan mayonnaise and gochujang paste and set aside.

Heat the oil in a frying pan/skillet, then add the marinated tempeh slices. Fry gently until they start to brown and become a little crispy on the outside; about 3–4 minutes on each side. Place on paper towels to drain.

To build your sandwich, layer the bottom slice of toasted bread with the lettuce and watercress, then top with the tomato slices. Generously drizzle with gochujang mayonnaise, then layer the fried tempeh slices over the top. Top with the second slice of toasted bread. Add a few pickled chillies/chiles if you like it with a bit more kick.

ROOT VEG ROSTI *with homemade beans*

We often used to eat rosti for breakfast while travelling in Sumatra, Indonesia. Although Swiss in origin, it was probably the Dutch who introduced the rosti into Indonesian food. During our European travels, it's been rare to find a rosti without ham, so I never got to taste the more delicate Swiss version with its crispy exterior and soft pillowy insides.

TO MAKE THE BEANS

450 g/2½ cups dried haricot/navy beans (or use half black-eyed beans/black-eyed peas)

2 tablespoons vegetable oil

1 celery stick, finely chopped

1 small carrot, peeled and finely chopped

2 garlic cloves, finely chopped

¼ teaspoon chilli/chili powder or 'magic dust' (see page 184, optional)

400-g/14-oz. can chopped tomatoes

2½ tablespoons tomato ketchup

1½ teaspoons cornflour/cornstarch

1½–2½ teaspoons salt, to taste

TO MAKE THE ROSTI

2 large potatoes, peeled and grated

½ small squash or 200 g/7 oz. pumpkin, peeled and grated

2 carrots, peeled and grated

2 tablespoons vegetable oil

1 large onion, finely sliced

½ tablespoon plain/all-purpose flour

½ tablespoon freshly chopped thyme (or ¼ teaspoon dried)

1–2 teaspoons salt, to taste

TO MAKE THE TEMPEH

250 g/9 oz. smoked tempeh or vegan 'ham/bacon'

1 teaspoon smoked paprika or mild paprika

½ teaspoon salt

½ tablespoon vegetable oil

SERVES 4–5

Soak the beans overnight in cold water. The next day, rinse with cold water and place in a medium pan with approximately 3 litres/12¾ cups water. Bring to the boil and simmer for 50 minutes until just softened.

Heat the oil in a deep frying pan/skillet, add the celery and carrot and sauté over low heat until softened and translucent. Add the garlic and cook for a further 2–3 minutes. Add all the remaining ingredients except the beans. Bring to the boil and then simmer for 20 minutes. Blitz the mixture with a hand blender, then add the beans and bring back to a simmer for a further 10–20 minutes, until the beans are soft. Set aside.

For the rosti, put the grated potatoes, squash and carrots into a large bowl. Pour over 2 litres/8½ cups boiling water and leave to stand for 10 minutes.

Heat 1 tablespoon of the oil in a frying pan/skillet and sauté the onion until it turns sticky. Add the flour and cook for a further 2–3 minutes. Tip the softened onion mixture into a large clean bowl.

Drain the grated vegetables, then, using your hands, squeeze out the excess water. (For the perfect rosti, and if you have time, you can refrigerate the grated part-cooked vegetables at this stage for a couple of hours.) Next, place the vegetables in a bowl with the softened onion. Add the thyme and salt to taste. Mix well.

Cut the tempeh into 1-cm/⅜-inch cubes. Place in a bowl with the paprika and salt, then mix well. Heat the oil in a small frying pan/skillet over moderately high heat. Fry the tempeh pieces until they are nicely browned and crispy. Drain on paper towels, then either add them to the beans or sprinkle on top of the beans at the end. Leave the beans over very low heat while finishing the rosti.

Place the frying pan/skillet back over medium heat with the remaining 1 tablespoon of oil. Scoop a large heaped tablespoon of the mixture into the pan and flatten with a spatula. Fry for 5–6 minutes on each side until golden. Place the rosti on a baking sheet and keep warm in a low oven (120°C (250°F) Gas ½) while frying the remaining rosti.

To assemble, place a cooked rosti or two on a plate, scoop two or three big spoonfuls of beans on top, and scatter with tempeh pieces.

CAULIFLOWER 'STEAK'
with green peppercorn sauce

Cauliflower is such a wonderfully versatile vegetable, with great texture and a full flavour that can be enhanced by roasting. Peppercorn steak is one of the first dishes I can remember ordering as a young child in a restaurant. It was never really about the beef for me, but about the warm and fragrant peppercorns. I'm quite obsessed with them these days. Kampot peppercorns from Cambodia are considered to be the best in the world. They are comparatively expensive but incredibly tasty when added to pickling juices (see Cambodian-style pickled vegetables, page 135). For this dish, green peppercorns are my absolute favourite after eating heaps of them in Thailand. They have a more fragrant warmth than their cousins, so they can be used more generously without becoming too harsh. You could use this sauce in lots of other dishes or as an alternative to gravy.

FOR THE GREEN PEPPERCORN SAUCE
2 tablespoons olive oil
2 banana shallots, finely chopped
1 teaspoon salt
½ teaspoon ground white pepper
1 tablespoon plain/all-purpose flour
1 litre/4¼ cups almond milk
80 ml/⅓ cup brandy (optional)
2 tablespoons green peppercorns, drained (or fresh, if possible)
200 ml/scant 1 cup vegan cream

FOR THE CAULIFLOWER 'STEAK'
1 large cauliflower, stem and leaves removed
4 tablespoons polenta/fine cornmeal
1 tablespoon nutritional yeast
½ teaspoon salt
1 teaspoon ground white pepper
1 teaspoon roughly ground black pepper
4 tablespoons pomace or vegetable oil

TO SERVE
chunky potato wedges

1 baking sheet, lightly oiled

SERVES 4

Preheat the oven to 200°C (400°F) Gas 6.

Start by making the sauce. Add the olive oil and the finely chopped shallots to a large frying pan/skillet. Place over medium heat and sauté until translucent and soft, but not coloured. Add the salt and white pepper. Add the flour and cook gently for 2–3 minutes, then slowly add the almond milk, whisking all the time to make a smooth sauce. Add the brandy (if using) and bring to a simmer for 4–5 minutes.

Roughly chop half of the green peppercorns. Add to the sauce along with the whole peppercorns. Add the cream and season to taste.

Wash and trim the cauliflower, and cut into four 2.5 cm/1 inch thick slices. In a bowl, mix together the polenta/fine cornmeal, nutritional yeast, salt and white and black pepper.

Rub the cauliflower steaks with the oil and then cover with the polenta/fine cornmeal mix. Place them on the lightly oiled baking sheet, and roast in the preheated oven for 15–20 minutes until crisp and golden.

Serve with chunky potato wedges, perfect for mopping up the moreish sauce.

MACADAMIA CRUMBLE POTS
with squash and chickpeas

Vegans and vegetarians often get asked the same questions and 'what do you eat for Christmas dinner?' is definitely one of the most common. For many years, I made Linda McCartney's Festive Roast from a recipe in her first cookbook. It remains a family favourite, over 20 years later. I particularly like any dish that can be prepared in advance, so these macadamia crumble pots are perfect for a stress-free dinner. If you are not keen on squash or pumpkin, you can substitute 250 g/9 oz. of chestnuts instead.

I try to include something seasonal and a bit luxurious in our Christmas dinner, and I think macadamia nuts are a special treat.

TO MAKE THE CRUMBLE TOPPING

120 g/scant 1 cup plain/all-purpose flour
80 g/scant 1 cup jumbo oats
1 teaspoon freshly chopped thyme
80 g/3 oz. vegan 'margarine', such as Stork, chopped into pieces
½ teaspoon salt
½ teaspoon white pepper
60 g/½ cup macadamia nuts

TO MAKE THE FILLING

1 squash, peeled and chopped into 2-cm/¾-inch cubes
1 tablespoon vegetable oil
1 small white onion, chopped
400-g/14-oz. can chickpeas/garbanzo beans, rinsed and drained
1 litre/4¼ cups vegetable stock
2 teaspoons Dijon mustard
250 g/9 oz. fresh spinach (or 100 g/3½ oz. frozen)
1 tablespoon freshly chopped thyme
4 fresh sage leaves, finely chopped
1 teaspoon cornflour/cornstarch
½–1 teaspoon salt, to taste
½ teaspoon white pepper

1 baking sheet, lightly oiled
5–6 individual pots

SERVES 5—6

Preheat the oven to 200°C (400°F) Gas 6.

Place the squash on the prepared baking sheet, drizzle over the oil and use your hands to ensure the pieces are well coated. Place in the preheated oven for 20–30 minutes, until it is golden brown with caramelized edges. Remove from the oven and reduce the temperature to 180°C (350°F) Gas 4, if you are planning to cook the pots immediately once prepared.

Meanwhile, prepare the crumble topping by placing the flour in a large bowl. Add the oats, thyme, salt and pepper, and mix well. Then add the margarine and, using your hands, rub the fat into the dry mixture to create a crumbly texture. Try to use the tips of your fingers so that the margarine doesn't go too soft. Roughly chop the macadamia nuts and add to the crumble. Mix well, then set aside.

In a large, deep frying pan/skillet or wok, sauté the onion for about 10–15 minutes over low heat until soft and translucent. Add the chickpeas/garbanzo beans, stock, mustard, spinach and herbs. Bring to a simmer for a few minutes.

Mix the cornflour/cornstarch in a little water and add to the pan, so that the mixture thickens slightly, then add the roasted squash, salt and pepper. Mix well and then taste to check the level of seasoning.

Fill the individual pots about three-quarters full with the roasted squash filling. Then top with a few tablespoons of the crumble mixture. If preparing in advance, the pots can be chilled or frozen at this stage.

To finish, place the pots on a baking sheet and bake in the preheated oven for 30–40 minutes until the crumble top is golden brown and the filling is starting to bubble underneath.

DEEP DIJON PIE *with olive oil mash*

Like most Northerners I love pie. But as much as I love a good cheese and onion pie, I wanted to make one that doesn't rely on dairy. Mustard is a global crowd-pleaser and Dijon is one of my favourites, making this creamy filling feel indulgent. I think pies should be indulgent. That's why I wanted it to have a good pastry-to-filling ratio, so a deep pie dish is absolutely essential.

The pastry for this satisfying deep-filled pie is based on Michel Roux's pâte brisée (see page 16, or you can just use ready-made vegan shortcrust pastry).

TO MAKE THE PIE

1 quantity vegan pastry (see page 16)

1 medium potato, peeled and diced

1 large carrot, peeled and diced

¼ cauliflower, cut into 1.5-cm/½-inch florets

3 tablespoons vegetable oil

1 heaped tablespoon plain/all-purpose flour, plus extra for dusting

350 ml/1½ cups almond milk

2 heaped tablespoons Dijon mustard

50 ml/3½ tablespoons almond cream

2 banana shallots, finely chopped

2 garlic cloves, minced

1 celery stick, diced

1 leek, sliced into 5-mm/¼-inch slices and washed

sea salt and white pepper, to taste

TO MAKE THE MASH

6–7 large Maris Piper or Yukon Gold potatoes, peeled and quartered

4–6 tablespoons good-quality virgin olive oil (I use Sicilian)

1–2 teaspoons rock or sea salt, to taste

1 teaspoon white pepper

TO SERVE

steamed greens and broccoli

1 deep pie dish or 4 individual pie dishes, oiled
baking beans

SERVES 4

Preheat the oven to 160°C (325°F) Gas 3.

If using four small pie dishes, divide the dough into four portions. Flour the surface and roll out the pastry to 3–4 mm/⅛ inch thick. Lay gently over the pie dish and gently but firmly push the pastry into the sides, ensuring there are no gaps or holes and the pastry hangs over the top of the dish. Trim the excess pastry but leave a 2-cm/¾-inch overhang to allow for shrinkage. Keep the trimmed pastry for making the pie tops later. Place in the fridge for 10–15 minutes.

Cover the pastry with a sheet of baking parchment and fill with baking beans. Bake for 20 minutes. The aim is to cook the pastry through without colouring if possible. Remove the baking parchment and beans and return the pastry to the oven for 5 minutes. Remove from the oven and set aside. Increase the oven temperature to 180°C (350°F) Gas 4.

To make the filling, parboil the potatoes for 10 minutes until just soft. Parboil the carrot and cauliflower for 3–4 minutes until just soft. Set aside.

Add 2 tablespoons of the vegetable oil to a deep frying pan/skillet and place over medium heat. Then add the flour and mix together to form a roux. Slowly add the almond milk, whisking constantly to make a thick, smooth white sauce. Add the Dijon mustard and almond cream and season with salt and white pepper to taste. Set aside.

Add the chopped shallots to a large pan, along with the remaining 1 tablespoon of vegetable oil. Fry for 5 minutes until just softened and translucent, then add the garlic, celery and leek and cook for another 3–4 minutes, until all the vegetables are well cooked and soft. Remove from the heat. Combine the shallot mixture with the parboiled vegetables and the creamy Dijon sauce. Mix well.

Fill the pastry case with the vegetable mixture. Roll out the remaining pastry on a well-floured surface and cut out one large round or four small rounds to fit the top of your pie dish(es). Brush the edges with almond milk and then use a fork to crimp the edges. Place the pie(s) on a baking sheet and bake for 20–25 minutes until the pastry is golden.

For the mash, boil the potatoes until soft; about 30 minutes. Drain in a colander for 5 minutes. Using a ricer or potato masher, mash the potatoes until smooth. Add olive oil, salt and pepper, and, using a whisk, whip the potatoes until creamy. Be careful not to over whip, or it will become gloopy. Taste to check the seasoning; add more salt if needed.

Serve the pies with the mash and steamed green beans and broccoli.

BLASKET BUNNY
Crusty soda bread filled with vegetable and Guinness stew

My father grew up in a small town in County Mayo on the north-west coast of Ireland. We've spent many family holidays exploring the west coast from the fishing village of Kinsale in the far south to the town of West Port, halfway up the coast. When I met Lee, I took him on a surprise trip to County Kerry, driving across Ireland in our neighbour's clapped-out Austin Metro in search of the Dingle Bay dolphin. We spotted him from the shoreline and swam out in the freezing January waters. And it was worth every single bone-freezing second.

I'm not going to lie; my experience of vegetarian food in Ireland has been outstandingly poor. Vegetarianism can present a cultural clash in an Irish family when it comes to food (and believe me I'm talking from experience here). Of course, there are big cream teas and enough eggs for breakfast to send off a small army, but I always wondered how long a vegan would survive in Ireland on root vegetables, soda bread and jam. It was only later during our Asian travels we realised that protein-packed peanut butter is an essential travel item (along with yeast extract and chilli/chili sauce). But there are a few Irish comfort staples I do love. Colcannon is definitely one of them – a delicious dish comprising mashed potato, fried cabbage and shallots, nearly always served with ham or bacon, although my step-mum makes it with eggs too.

Then there is Guinness. Possibly Ireland's most famous export, rich in iron and nationally declared as 'Good For You', this velvety Irish stout with its complex, deep, burnt barley taste brings some serious flavours to the party. I can still remember finding out it wasn't vegetarian when I was in my late teens (along with a whole host of other enjoyable alcoholic beverages). When the company decided to make it vegan in early 2015, I celebrated by making a vegetable and Guinness stew. I have given it a street food twist here, but you can serve this with dumplings or celeriac mash for something a little bit lighter.

Bunny Chow hails from South Africa, and was usually some kind of loaf or roll, hollowed out and filled with a spiced stew or dal. This is an Irish version of that, taking its name from the Blasket islands off the coast of County Kerry. Making soda bread is supposed to be the easiest of bread recipes, but you can always cheat and buy one. It's all about the stew really.

Blasket Islands, County Kerry.

FOR THE SODA BREAD

800 g/6 cups wholemeal/whole-wheat flour

1½ teaspoons bicarbonate of soda/baking soda

1½ teaspoons fine rock salt

3 teaspoons lemon juice

750 ml/3 cups almond milk

handful of coarse polenta/cornmeal, for sprinkling

FOR THE STEW

2 tablespoons vegetable oil

2 celery sticks, finely chopped

4 small white onions, 2 finely chopped and 2 sliced

500 g/1 lb. 2 oz. chestnut or button mushrooms, cleaned and halved

1 tablespoon plain/all-purpose flour

600 ml/2½ cups Guinness

400 g/14 oz. waxy potatoes, peeled and cut into 2.5-cm/1-inch chunks

2 large carrots, peeled and thickly sliced

2 turnips, peeled and diced into 2.5-cm/1-inch chunks

½ small swede/rutabaga, peeled and diced into 2.5-cm/1-inch chunks

½ teaspoon mustard powder

2 tablespoons dark soy sauce

1 teaspoon yeast extract or ½ tablespoon tomato purée/paste

2 tablespoons good-quality vegetable stock

2 bay leaves

1 sprig of thyme

1–2 teaspoons salt, to taste

handful of freshly chopped thyme, to serve

1 baking sheet, lightly oiled

SERVES 4

Preheat the oven to 200°C (400°F) Gas 6. Add a tablespoon of polenta/cornmeal to the oiled baking sheet and shake it until it is well covered.

To prepare the soda bread, place the flour in a large bowl, add the bicarbonate of soda/baking soda and salt, then mix well. In a jug/pitcher, combine the lemon juice and almond milk. Pour the liquid into the flour and gently knead together for no more than a minute or two to make a soft dough. Divide the dough into four pieces and roll each to form a small ball. Place on the prepared baking sheet and cut a cross into the top of each ball, about 1 cm/⅜ inch deep. Bake in the preheated oven for 15–20 minutes until the soda bread is lightly browned. Tap the bottom to check the sound is hollow.

For the stew, heat the oil in a large heavy-bottomed pan over high heat. Add the finely chopped celery sticks, the two finely chopped onions and four of the mushrooms, finely chopped (the rest of the onions and mushrooms will be added later). Sauté over medium heat until dark golden brown and well caramelized.

Add the flour to the softened mixture and mix well, cooking gently for 2–3 minutes. Pour in the Guinness and mix well, scraping up any browned bits from the bottom of the pan to make a rich roux. Add the remaining ingredients and bring to the boil, then simmer uncovered for about 40–50 minutes until all the vegetables are fully cooked.

Slice the top off the cooled soda breads and scoop out the middle. Serve the vegetable stew inside the hollowed-out bread and top with the soda bread lid and a handful of freshly chopped thyme.

ITAL STEW *with cumin-spiced Johnny cakes*

This is a Caribbean punchy broth with vegetables and dumplings. I started making an Ital-style stew to make me feel less guilty about the accompanying dumplings, especially after I discovered that the dough tastes even better when fried. The Johnny cakes, traditional West Indian dumplings, are part-baked to avoid absorbing too much oil from frying. You can roll the dough into finger shapes and drop them straight into the stew (spinner dumplings) if you want to avoid frying. Ital, from the word 'vital', is a style of Rastafarian cooking focused on food that increases energy (livity) and is mostly plant-based. See page 38–39 for the accompaniments and recipe image.

TO MAKE THE JOHNNY CAKES (DUMPLINGS)

- 300 g/2¼ cups plain/all-purpose flour
- 1 teaspoon cumin seeds, lightly toasted
- 1 teaspoon salt
- 3 teaspoons baking powder
- 120 g/4 oz. coconut butter or vegan baking margarine, chopped
- 180 ml/¾ cup water
- 120 ml/½ cup pomace or vegetable oil

TO MAKE THE STEW

- 2 tablespoons pomace oil
- 1 white onion, roughly chopped
- 6 spring onions/scallions, sliced (whites and green parts separated)
- 4–5 fat garlic cloves
- ½ teaspoon whole allspice
- 2 carrots, peeled and cut into 2-cm/¾-inch chunks
- 1 cho cho or turnip, peeled and cut into 2-cm/¾-inch chunks
- 2 waxy potatoes, peeled and cut into 2-cm/¾-inch chunks
- ½–1 Scotch Bonnet chilli/chile, finely chopped, to taste
- ½ butternut squash, peeled and cut into 2-cm/¾-inch chunks
- 400 g/14-oz can gungo peas or chickpeas/garbanzo beans, drained and rinsed
- small handful of freshly chopped thyme (or 1 teaspoon dried)
- 2 bay leaves
- 1.5 litres/6¼ cups vegetable stock
- 400-ml/14-oz. can good-quality coconut milk

TO SERVE

- crispy jerk skins (see page 38)
- Dougie's hot habanero sauce (see page 38)
- handful of fresh coriander/cilantro, roughly chopped
- squeeze of fresh lime juice

SERVES 4

For the dumplings, combine the flour, cumin, salt and baking powder and rub in the coconut butter to make a crumb. Slowly add the water to make a dough. Knead slightly until smooth, then wrap in clingfilm/plastic wrap and chill for 20–30 minutes.

Divide the dough into eight balls. If you do not want to fry the dumplings, roll them into cigar shapes and drop into boiling water about 15 minutes before the vegetables are fully cooked, then drain and add the dumplings to the stew just before serving.

To part-fry and part-bake the dumplings, preheat the oven to 165°C (325°F) Gas 3. Place a pan with the oil over medium-high heat until a small crumb of bread or dough sizzles immediately but doesn't burn. Fry the dumplings for 2 minutes on each side until lightly browned. Drain on paper towels, then place on a baking sheet and transfer to the preheated oven. Bake for 10–15 minutes; the dumplings will puff up more. Keep on low in the oven until the stew is ready.

Heat the pomace oil in a pan, add the onion, white parts of the spring onions/scallions, garlic, allspice, carrots and cho cho. Sauté for a few minutes, then add the stock and 570 ml/2½ cups water. Bring to the boil and simmer for 8 minutes. Add the remaining ingredients except the green parts of the spring onions/scallions. Simmer for 20–30 minutes until the vegetables are cooked. Add the spring onion/scallion greens and serve with the dumplings, crispy jerk skins, hot sauce, coriander/cilantro and a squeeze of lime.

Dougie's hot habanero sauce

A simple and delicious habanero jerk sauce that you can make as spicy as you like! I love West Indian food, which is often hailed as the definition of soul food and the home of comfort food recipes. There is an iconic West Indian café called Dougie's in Manchester's infamous Moss Side, from where we used to pick up our rice, peas and dumplings, smothered in Dougie's hot sauce for lunch. It was carb-filled vegan eating at its early '90s best. Times have changed. Dougie's has long gone and the dilapidated building has been demolished. But that habanero jerk sauce will never be forgotten.

2 tablespoons olive oil
2 banana shallots, finely chopped
½–2 habanero chillies/chiles, finely chopped, to taste
1 teaspoon mild paprika
½ teaspoon dried thyme (or 1 tablespoon freshly chopped)
½ teaspoon ground allspice
⅓ teaspoon ground cloves
180 ml/¾ cup orange juice
3 tablespoons fresh lime juice
1 teaspoon unrefined brown sugar
1–2 teaspoons salt, to taste
½ teaspoon white pepper

MAKES 250 ML/1 CUP

Heat the oil in small saucepan over medium-high heat. Sauté the shallots for about 6–8 minutes until translucent and soft.

Add the chillies/chiles, paprika, thyme, allspice and cloves, and sauté for 1 minute. Add the orange juice, lime juice and sugar, and simmer for 10–15 minutes. Season with salt and white pepper. This sauce will keep for up to a week in a clean jar in the fridge.

Crispy jerk skins

These jerk-spiced crispy bean curd skins have a delicious crunch and are so super quick and easy to prepare, you'll want to make them time and again. Bean curd skin is a great textured vegetable protein that will absorb all the flavours you add. It can be cooked until soft or baked until crispy, and comes in sticks or sheets (which can be twisted into knots when softened). The peas are usually a type of bean called gungo, and are easy to find in West Indian grocery stores, or you can use kidney beans which are more readily available and far cheaper. I serve these alongside the Ital stew and Johnny cakes (see page 37) for a West Indian-inspired vegan banquet.

200 g/7 oz. dried bean curd sticks (small type) or skins, soaked in hot water for 20 minutes
2 tablespoons jerk seasoning
½ teaspoon salt
1 tablespoon pomace oil

1 baking sheet, lightly oiled

SERVES 4

Preheat the oven to 165°C (325°F) Gas 3.

Drain the bean curd sticks or sheets and lay on paper towels to dry slightly. Tip into a bowl and add the jerk seasoning, salt and oil. Using your hands, mix well ensuring all the bean curd is well covered. Set aside.

Lay the bean curd sticks onto the prepared baking sheet. If using bean curd sheets, gently twist the sheet and tie into a knot, to make a little knotted stick. Bake in the preheated oven for 15–20 minutes until crispy and golden.

BAKED BEETROOT
and horseradish Mornay

I love beetroot/beets. So did Tom Robbins it seems. He wrote a series of weird and wonderful books in the '80s and '90s (remember *Even Cowgirls Get the Blues* and Uma Thurman with her giant thumbs for hitchhiking?). One of my favourite of Robbins' books had an entire chapter dedicated to the wonders of beetroot/beets: 'The beet is the most intense of vegetables. The radish, admittedly, is more feverish, but the fire of the radish is a cold fire, the fire of discontent not of passion. Tomatoes are lusty enough, yet there runs through tomatoes an undercurrent of frivolity. Beets are deadly serious.' *Jitterbug Perfume* (1984).

According to Tom, it could be the secret to immortality. I'm not sure about that, but I have noticed its resurgence on dining menus. This is a lovely accompaniment for a traditional Sunday dinner.

6 yellow and red beetroots/beets
1 litre/4¼ cups almond milk
2 bay leaves
7.5–10-cm/3–4-inch root of horseradish, peeled and grated (or 2 tablespoons horseradish sauce from a jar)
3 tablespoons pomace oil
2 heaped tablespoons plain/all-purpose flour
2 tablespoons nutritional yeast
1–2 teaspoons rock salt, to taste
½ teaspoon white pepper
2 tablespoons cashew cream (see page 12)
1 slice brown or rye bread, blitzed to rough breadcrumbs
1 tablespoon pumpkin seeds
½ tablespoon sunflower seeds
1 tablespoon vegan Italian-style hard cheese

SERVES 4–5

Top and tail the beetroots/beets (do not peel) and place in large pan of boiling water. Simmer for 30–40 minutes until fully cooked. Remove from the pan and set aside to cool.

Preheat the oven to 190°C (375°F) Gas 5.

In a small pan, heat the milk gently and add the bay leaves and grated horseradish. Bring to a gentle simmer, then remove from the heat and leave to poach.

In a deep frying pan/skillet, heat the pomace oil over medium heat. Add the flour and whisk to make a roux, cooking gently for 2–3 minutes. Strain the milk into a jug/pitcher, then pour slowly into the roux, a little at a time, whisking constantly until all the milk is combined and you have a thick and creamy sauce. Keep over low heat and add the nutritional yeast, salt and pepper. Add the cashew cream and stir well, then remove the sauce from the heat.

Using gloved hands, use your fingers to rub the peel from the cooked beetroot/beets. Then slice the beetroot/beets into 5 mm/¼ inch thick discs.

Layer the beetroot/beet slices in a deep ovenproof dish, and pour over the Mornay sauce. Sprinkle the breadcrumbs, seeds and cheese over the top, then bake for 20–25 minutes until the top is golden and bubbling. Serve immediately.

SAVOY-WRAPPED *quinoa roast*

This is another great vegan roast, perfect for a traditional family or Sunday dinner, and it can be made with or without the vegan cheese (although the salty layer makes a flavoursome contrast to the filling). Serve with all the usual trimmings of course. Roast potatoes with rosemary, creamy mash (I like to mix it with spinach, but I also started making carrot and potato mash after my teen daughter decided she no longer liked cooked carrots), minted peas and homemade onion gravy. Don't be put off by the savoy wrapping. Simply remove the thick part of the lower stem, and blanch it well in the potato water. Be generous with the overlapping layers to ensure it holds together.

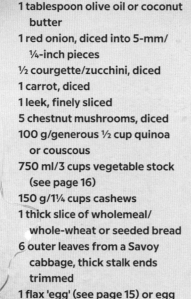

1 tablespoon olive oil or coconut butter

1 red onion, diced into 5-mm/ ¼-inch pieces

½ courgette/zucchini, diced

1 carrot, diced

1 leek, finely sliced

5 chestnut mushrooms, diced

100 g/generous ½ cup quinoa or couscous

750 ml/3 cups vegetable stock (see page 16)

150 g/1¼ cups cashews

1 thick slice of wholemeal/ whole-wheat or seeded bread

6 outer leaves from a Savoy cabbage, thick stalk ends trimmed

1 flax 'egg' (see page 15) or egg replacer

120 g/4 oz. silken tofu

1 tablespoon freshly chopped thyme and marjoram (or ½ teaspoon dried herbs)

120 g/4 oz. vegan 'feta' or 'ricotta' (see page 15, optional)

salt and white pepper, to taste

loaf pan, oiled

SERVES 6

Preheat the oven to 190°C (375°F) Gas 5.

Heat the oil or coconut butter in a pan and add the onion, courgette/zucchini, carrot, leek and mushrooms. Cook for 8–10 minutes until soft.

Simmer the quinoa for 4–5 minutes in vegetable stock. Drain and set aside.

Toast the cashews in a dry frying pan/skillet, then bash (or blitz in a food processor) into small pieces. Avoid over-blitzing the nuts to a powder or you will lose the texture. Blitz the bread into crumbs. Blanche the cabbage leaves for 2 minutes. Set aside.

Mix the vegetables, nuts, breadcrumbs, flax 'egg' and tofu together. Add the fresh or dried herbs and season to taste with salt and white pepper.

Line the loaf pan with the cabbage leaves, using five large leaves to cover the bottom and saving one leaf to seal the top. Half-fill the loaf pan with half of the mixture, firmly pushing it down with the back of a spoon. Crumble the vegan cheese (if using) over the filling, then add the remaining filling on top, again pushing down to create a firm shape.

Fold over the edges of the leaves to cover the top of the roast, and then place the last leaf on top and tuck it into the sides. Cover the pan with foil and place on a baking sheet. Bake in the preheated oven for 15 minutes, then turn over, foil-side down on the baking sheet, and bake for 10–15 minutes more.

Turn it the right way up again and remove the foil lid. Turn it out onto a board and serve.

MY BIG FAT *veggie cottage pie*

This was one of the first recipes I ever posted on my blog following MasterChef, and it has continued to have the highest page visits ever since. My big fat veggie cottage pie has been our family comfort dish of choice for several decades now. It's a healthy, hearty and delicious dish that will satisfy the whole family (and warm a few cockles in the process). We always eat this with pickled red cabbage or beetroot/beets, but any other pickled vegetable would be equally tasty. You could replace the potato topping for sweet potato or celeriac mash if you wanted to give this dish a healthier twist.

TO MAKE THE MASH

8–10 large Maris Piper or Yukon Gold potatoes, peeled and quartered

3–4 tablespoons virgin olive oil (I use Sicilian)

sea salt and black pepper

2 tablespoons almond cream (optional)

TO MAKE THE FILLING

2 tablespoons pomace or vegetable oil

2 large onions, cut into 1.5-cm/½-inch chunks

3 garlic cloves, crushed and chopped

1 celery stick, cut into 1-cm/⅜-inch chunks

2 tablespoons plain/all-purpose flour

2 large carrots, cut into 1.5-cm/½-inch chunks

2 leeks, sliced and washed

3 large field mushrooms, cut into 2-cm/¾-inch chunks (or other mushrooms of choice)

850 ml/3½ cups vegetable stock (see page 16)

2 tablespoons dark soy sauce

1 teaspoon yeast extract

small handful of fresh thyme

small sprig of rosemary (rubbed between fingers to release flavour)

2 bay leaves

450 g/1 lb. soya or tofu mince (or use an extra 200 g/7 oz. green lentils)

150 g/5 oz. green lentils, simmered in water for 1 hour until soft

125 g/1 generous cup frozen peas

sea salt and white pepper

TO SERVE

pickled red cabbage (optional)

SERVES 5–6

To make the mash, boil the potatoes in a large pan until soft; about 30 minutes. Drain in a colander for 5 minutes. Using a ricer or potato masher, smash the potatoes until well mashed and smooth. Add the olive oil, salt, pepper and almond cream, if using, and mash again. Set aside.

Preheat the oven to 190°C (375°F) Gas 5.

For the filling, heat the oil in a pan and sauté the onions, garlic and celery until they start to soften. Add the flour and stir well to make a little roux, then add the remaining vegetables and mix well.

Add the stock, soy sauce, yeast extract, fresh herbs and bay leaves and mix again, while bringing to the boil. Once the vegetables start to soften, add the vegan mince and cooked lentils, stirring well.

Bring to the boil, add salt and white pepper to taste, and then simmer on low for 20–30 minutes, allowing the mixture to reduce slightly to a thick gravy. Add the frozen peas and cook for another 5 minutes.

Transfer the mixture to a large, deep ovenproof dish, aiming for at least 5-cm/2-inch depth of mixture. Layer the creamy mashed potatoes over the top. You want about twice as much filling to mash.

Bake in the preheated oven until bubbling and the top is golden and crispy.

CAULIFLOWER MAC 'N' JACK
with crispy caper bites

The British staple of cauliflower cheese is often considered the ultimate way to serve cauliflower. But what do you do if you can't decide whether to have cauliflower cheese or macaroni cheese? My friend Jo said they just have both together, problem solved. So, we adopted this idea without any hesitation! It was one of the hardest dishes to 'let go of' from my vegetarian diet, but then I was introduced to nutritional yeast, and discovered I could still enjoy a gooey, rich and warming vegan version without bothering any cows.

1 cauliflower, cut into large florets

200 g/7 oz. macaroni or penne pasta

1 litre/4¼ cups almond milk

2 bay leaves

few sprigs of fresh thyme

3 tablespoons pomace or vegetable oil

2 heaped tablespoons plain/all-purpose flour

4–5 heaped tablespoons nutritional yeast

3 teaspoons English/hot mustard (or 2 teaspoons mustard powder)

2 teaspoons onion powder

1 teaspoon sweet smoked paprika

1–2 teaspoons rock salt

½ teaspoon white pepper

100 g/generous ¾ cup cashews, soaked in water for 2 hours and blended to a fine paste

60–120 ml/¼–½ cup Jack Daniels (or other whiskey, optional)

1 tablespoon grated vegan Italian-style hard cheese (optional)

TO MAKE THE CRISPY CAPER BITES

1–2 tablespoons capers or green olives, roughly chopped

1 tablespoon cornflour/cornstarch

1–2 teaspoons rock salt

vegetable oil, for frying

large baking sheet, lightly oiled

SERVES 4–5

Preheat the oven to 220°C (425°F) Gas 7.

Place the cauliflower florets on the oiled baking sheet and bake in the hot oven for 20 minutes until starting to turn golden and brown.

Cook the pasta according to the packet instructions, but minus 4 minutes, as the pasta will finish cooking when it is baked at the end. This way, it won't be overcooked and mushy. Keep some the cooking water for later.

In a small pan, heat the milk gently with the bay leaves and sprigs of thyme. Bring to a gentle simmer, then remove from the heat and leave the herbs to poach.

In a deep frying pan/skillet, heat the pomace oil over medium heat. Add the flour and whisk to make a roux, cooking gently for 2–3 minutes. Strain the milk into a jug/pitcher, then pour slowly into the roux, a little at a time, whisking constantly over low heat until all the milk is combined and you have a thick and creamy sauce. Keep over low heat and add the nutritional yeast, mustard, onion powder, paprika, salt and pepper. Add the blended cashews and Jack Daniels, then stir well. Remove from the heat.

Mix the cooked pasta and the sauce together. Then carefully add the cauliflower florets and mix well. There should be plenty of sauce, so add some of the pasta liquid if needed. Tip into a large baking dish.

To make the crispy caper bites, drain the capers or olives, then lay on paper towels to dry slightly. Mix together the cornflour/cornstarch and salt, and toss the capers in the seasoned flour. In a small pan, heat the vegetable oil over medium-high heat. Check the oil is hot enough by dropping in one piece – it should sizzle immediately without burning. Gently add the capers to the pan and fry until crisp and golden. Drain on paper towels.

Sprinkle the crispy caper bites over the top of the cauliflower pasta. Season with a sprinkle of salt and black pepper over the top, and add a sprinkling of vegan cheese, if using.

LOADED PIEROGI
with mushrooms and sauerkraut

Pierogi remind me of the Tibetan momo (stuffed dumplings). Indeed, they may well have some Chinese heritage. The simplicity of an unleavened dough stuffed with savoury or sweet fillings (just like momos) is very appealing. The focus of the filling is always on what's local and seasonal, making it a cheap and accessible dish to make, and probably why it has travelled so far and wide across Eurasia. I've tried Canadian-Ukrainian versions in Vancouver and Polish pierogi in my local markets. I really love the 'loaded' style of serving, where toppings are piled onto the dumplings.

I think learning to pickle and ferment vegetables are important skills, and I have recently fallen in love with *Pickled* by Freddie Jansen. It truly is the best way to make the most of seasonal gluts. But in our time-pressed Western world we always have a fall-back, and fortunately sauerkraut is cheap and widely available.

TO MAKE THE DOUGH
400 g/3 cups plain/all-purpose flour
1 tablespoon olive oil
1 teaspoon salt
250 ml/1 cup hand-hot water

TO MAKE THE FILLING
2 tablespoons olive oil
2 shallots, finely chopped
240 g/8½ oz. wild mushrooms (or 120 g/4 oz. dried)
3 tablespoons simple sauerkraut, drained (see page 191)
½–1 teaspoon rock salt
½ teaspoon ground black pepper

TO MAKE THE TOPPING
2 banana shallots, roughly chopped
splash of olive oil
2 tablespoons maple tempeh 'bacon', diced (see page 25)
2 tablespoons cashew cream, thick (see page 12)
½ teaspoon white pepper
½ teaspoon salt

SERVES 3–4

Combine the ingredients for the dough, kneading until well combined and smooth; this will take at least 5–6 minutes. Place in an oiled bowl and cover. Set aside in a warm place for at least an hour.

Fill a deep pan with water and a splash of vegetable oil. This will stop the pierogi sticking to each other when boiled.

To make the filling, heat the oil in a small frying pan/skillet and sauté the finely chopped shallots for 3–4 minutes, then add the chopped mushrooms. Season with the salt and black pepper. Sauté for 4–5 minutes until well cooked. Set aside in a bowl.

For the topping, in the same pan, cook the roughly chopped banana shallots with a splash of olive oil and fry for 8–10 minutes until they are browning nicely. Then add the tempeh pieces and fry for another minute or two. Season with the salt and pepper, and then set aside.

Roll out the dough on a well-floured surface. Using an 8–10-cm/3–4-inch cookie cutter, cut out discs, ensuring they don't stick to each other.

To make the dumplings, place a dough disc in one hand and add ½ tablespoon of the mushroom filling. Add a generous pinch of sauerkraut. Fold over the disc, forming a half-moon shape. Seal the edge with water and pinch together. When all the dumplings are wrapped, add them to the pan of boiling water and cook for about 5–6 minutes until they float to the surface and the dough is translucent. The dumplings can be served straight from the pan, or you can lightly fry them in a splash of olive oil to add a little crispness to the pastry.

Once cooked, layer onto a plate. Top the dumplings with smatterings of fried onions, tempeh pieces and generous drizzles of cashew cream.

JERUSALEM ARTICHOKES
with garlic cream and hazelnut crust

I tend to be led by flavours in food first rather than their health-giving properties, but it's always a small joy to find out something I love is also very good for me. And I do love hazelnuts. This dish is rich and unctuous, and feels like a treat especially when served with crusty bread and steamed broccoli. The creamy cauliflower sauce works well with pasta for a carbonara-style sauce, or serve this dish alongside a savoy-wrapped quinoa roast (see page 42) and crispy roast potatoes for a big traditional dinner.

1 kg/2 lb. 4 oz. Jerusalem
    artichokes
4 shallots
6 garlic cloves, left whole
½ cauliflower, cut into florets
1–2 tablespoons olive oil
1 teaspoon white pepper
425 ml/1¾ cups almond milk or
    other vegan milk, plus extra
    if needed
2 tablespoons lemon juice
½ teaspoon mustard powder
1 teaspoon onion powder
1 teaspoon salt
1 slice brown or rye bread,
    blitzed to rough breadcrumbs
3 tablespoons panko breadcrumbs
1 tablespoon freshly chopped
    marjoram or parsley (or
    ½ teaspoon dried)
2 tablespoons toasted hazelnuts,
    roughly chopped

SERVES 4–6

Peel the Jerusalem artichokes and slice into 5 mm/¼ inch thick discs. Set aside in salted water to prevent them discolouring.

Preheat the oven to 220°C (425°F) Gas 7.

Lay the shallots, garlic and cauliflower florets on a baking sheet and drizzle with half the olive oil. Season with half the pepper and toss slightly. Lay the Jerusalem artichokes on another baking sheet, drizzle with the rest of the olive oil and season with the remaining pepper. Place both baking sheets in the hot oven and roast for about 30 minutes until the cauliflower and artichokes are tender.

Transfer all the roasted vegetables to a food processor or blender, add the almond milk, lemon juice, mustard powder, onion powder and salt. Blitz until very smooth. Add more milk if necessary, to make a smooth, pourable sauce. Adjust the seasoning to taste if needed.

Layer the Jerusalem artichokes in a deep baking dish and then pour over the sauce. Sprinkle both type of breadcrumbs, the herbs and chopped hazelnuts over the top. Place in the hot oven for about 20–30 minutes until golden on top and bubbling. Serve immediately.

BAKE O'RAMA'S *chocolate cake*

There's nothing quite like a slice of fudgy, bittersweet chocolate cake to satisfy that simultaneous cake and cocoa craving. And everyone needs a fool-proof recipe for chocolate cake perfection, whether you're vegan or not. This cake was one of the biggest selling cakes in a popular diner in Manchester's Northern Quarter, and most people didn't even realise they were eating a vegan cake. Manchester's mistress of cake creations Bake O'Rama, aka Charlotte O'Toole, has now joined forces with other local legends, Ginger's Comfort Emporium and Lush Brownies to open Manchester's first dessert café, MilkJam. I haven't changed a thing from the recipe, other than quartering the ingredients, but like many of Charlotte's creations this cake is still massive – halve the quantities if you want something a bit smaller. Serve with a big mug of tea.

490 ml/2 cups soy milk

1½ teaspoons cider vinegar

135 ml/½ cup plus 1 tablespoon vegetable oil

300 g/1¼ cups caster/granulated sugar

240 g/2 cups self-raising/self-rising flour

100 g/1 cup unsweetened cocoa powder

½ teaspoon bicarbonate of soda/baking soda

½ teaspoon baking powder

TO MAKE THE BUTTERCREAM

600 g/1 lb. 5 oz. vegan margarine

300 g/2 cups icing/confectioners' sugar

4 tablespoons soy or almond milk

75 g/¾ cup unsweetened cocoa powder

TO MAKE THE GANACHE

400 ml/1 ¾ cups vegan cream

225 g/8 oz. 70% cocoa vegan chocolate, broken into pieces

TO DECORATE

chocolate shavings (optional)

4 15-cm/6-inch cake pans, oiled and lined

SERVES 8–10

Preheat the oven to 180°C (350°F) Gas 4.

Mix together the soy milk, vinegar, vegetable oil and sugar in a large bowl. Leave to curdle for 5 minutes.

Sift the flour, cocoa, bicarbonate of soda/baking soda and baking powder three times to aerate and remove any lumps.

Mix together the dry and wet ingredients gradually, but quickly. Make sure there are no lumps and the batter is smooth. Pour evenly into the four cake pans. Place in the preheated oven immediately and bake until they are evenly risen and cooked through, about 25–30 minutes. Remove from the oven and cool completely.

To make the chocolate buttercream, mix together all the ingredients using a handheld electric whisk until creamy and light. Using a palette knife or metal spatula, stack the sponges, layering them generously with buttercream,

and then lightly cover the outside of the whole cake, so you can still see some of the lines for the sponge layers. Place in the fridge to chill.

Meanwhile, make the ganache. Place the cream in a pan and bring to boil. Remove from the heat and pour over the chocolate pieces in a heatproof bowl. Whisk until smooth and the chocolate has melted, then generously pour over the top of the layered cakes allowing the ganache to run down the sides. If, like me you lack piping skills, you can simply decorate with chocolate shavings. Or you can pipe some of the leftover buttercream on top and add whatever decorations you like.

PLUM AND PISTACHIO CRUMBLE
with star anise custard

I make this crumble all the time at home, alternating the filling with rhubarb, as I now grow both fruits in my garden. When I was 10, I would ride my pony under the massive plum trees growing over the neighbouring farm wall, and fill my pockets before setting off for a day's ride out. I'm always happy to find out that something I love to eat is easy to grow at home. I would add courgettes/zucchini, kale and rocket/arugula to that list, all of which can be grown in a tub. I'm not naturally green-fingered and have learned to grow vegetables and fruit by trial and error.

2 kg/4½ lb. plums, washed and stoned/pitted, halved (or quartered if they are very large)

6 Indonesian long peppercorns (or 6 cloves)

2 tablespoons unrefined brown sugar

1 teaspoon ground cinnamon

TO MAKE THE CRUMBLE

250 g/scant 2 cups plain/all-purpose flour

180 g/6½ oz. vegetable margarine

120 g/1¼ cups jumbo oats

100 g/½ cup unrefined brown sugar

80 g/¾ cup pistachios, roughly chopped

TO MAKE THE CUSTARD

570 ml/scant 2½ cups soy or almond milk, plus a splash extra

3–4 star anise, roughly ground so that the seeds are crushed slightly

1 vanilla pod/bean, split

1½ tablespoons cornflour/cornstarch

about 120 ml/½ cup soy or almond cream, to taste

about 2 tablespoons unrefined light brown sugar, to taste

SERVES 6

Preheat the oven to 190°C (375°F) Gas 5.

Layer the plums and Indonesian peppercorns into a deep baking dish, and sprinkle with the sugar and cinnamon powder.

To make the crumble, sift the flour into a large bowl and add the margarine. Rub together with your finger tips to make a breadcrumb-like texture, then add the oats, sugar and pistachios. Mix well and layer on top of the plums. Bake in the preheated oven for 35–45 minutes until bubbling and the crumble is golden brown.

To make the custard, bring the milk to a gentle boil together with the star anise. Scrape in the seeds from the vanilla pod/bean and then add the scraped pod/bean as well. Simmer gently for 5 minutes, then remove from the heat and set aside for 15–20 minutes while the flavours infuse.

Mix together the cornflour/cornstarch with the extra splash of cold milk to make a paste. Strain the infused milk to remove any large bits. Whisk the cornflour/cornstarch paste into the warm milk and return to the heat. Bring to a simmer again for a few minutes. Add the almond cream and sugar to taste. Remove from the heat. If not using immediately, cover the surface with clingfilm/plastic wrap to stop a skin forming. Serve the crumble in bowls with a ladle or two of warm custard.

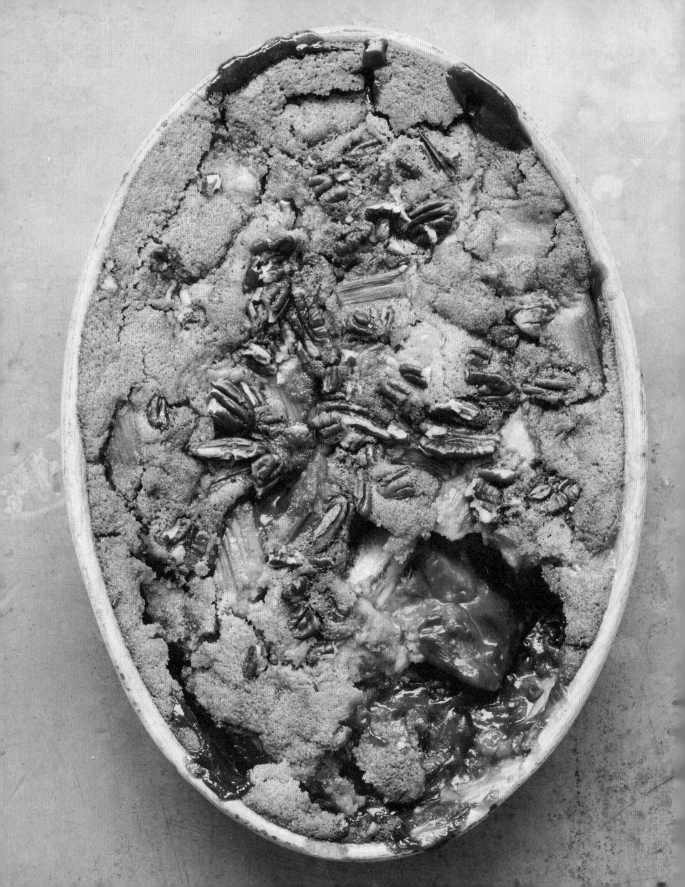

STICKY TOFFEE
and rhubarb pudding

I made this dessert one Sunday for my dairy-loving extended family and no-one realised they were eating a plant-powered pudding. The basic recipe is based on one I learned from one of Nigella's early books, which is an easy, no-mess sticky toffee pudding. The addition of rhubarb (or apples) brings a delicious tart edge alongside the sticky sweet sauce.

140 g/1 cup self-raising/self-rising flour

100 g/½ cup unrefined light brown sugar

1 tablespoon baking powder

pinch of salt

200 ml/scant 1 cup almond milk

85 g/3 oz. vegan margarine

1 flax 'egg' (see page 15) or egg replacer

scraped seeds from ½ vanilla pod/bean (or 1 teaspoon vanilla extract)

8 sticks of rhubarb

140 g/scant ¾ cup unrefined dark brown sugar

50 g/scant ½ cup pecans

TO SERVE
vegan ice-cream (see page 58)

deep baking dish, oiled

SERVES 6

Preheat the oven to 180°C (350°F) Gas 4.

In a large bowl, mix the flour, light brown sugar, baking powder and salt.

Mix together the almond milk, margarine, flax 'egg', tofu and vanilla seeds. Add to the dry ingredients and mix well to make a smooth batter.

Arrange the rhubarb in the prepared baking dish and pour the batter over the top of the fruit. Smooth across the fruit to ensure the rhubarb is well covered. In a small bowl, mix 250 ml/1 cup boiling water with the unrefined dark brown sugar until dissolved. Pour over the batter mixture, then scatter the pecans across the top. Bake in the preheated oven for about 40 minutes until the pudding has risen and is golden brown on top.

Use a big spoon to serve, making sure each bowl has an even mix of sponge, fruit and toffee sauce. Serve with vegan ice-cream.

GINGER'S VANILLA MALT *ice-cream*

I've met some amazing people over the years through my involvement in MasterChef and my journey into British street food. I've learned from some fantastic producers and restaurateurs, and I'm particularly indebted to Claire Kelsey, three-time British Street Food Award winner including Best of the Best at BSFA 2012 with her Ginger's Comfort Emporium ice-cream for grown-ups. The peanut butter and jelly ice-cream is one of those astounding flavours that defies any vegan put-downs. If that's not a good enough reason to visit Manchester, I don't know what is.

This recipe is another Ginger's favourite and perfect for serving alongside different desserts, including the sticky toffee and rhubarb pudding (see page 57). Hot and cold together in a dessert is a joyful childhood memory, where it had to be a very special treat to be having cake AND ice-cream at the same time!

600 ml/2½ cups soy milk
400 ml/1¾ cups full-fat
    coconut milk
175 g/scant 1 cup sugar
1 fair-trade vanilla
    pod/bean, halved
    lengthways and seeds
    scraped

135 g/5 oz. malt powder
60 g/2 oz. coconut oil
½ teaspoon guar or
    xanthan gum (unless
    you intend to eat
    straight after churning)

MAKES 1 LITRE/1 QUART

Warm the milks in a pan over medium heat. Add the sugar, vanilla seeds and pod/bean, malt powder and coconut oil. Gently whisk on low so that the oil melts and the malt powder gets cooked out, about 5 minutes.

Let it cool, remove the vanilla pod/bean and then add the guar gum or xanthan gum. It needs to be incorporated with a hand blender until the mixture is completely smooth.

Churn the ice-cream in an ice-cream maker according to the manufacturer's instructions. If you don't have an in ice-cream churner, pour the mixture into a large sealable tub and place in the freezer.

The ice-cream will keep for several months in the freezer. Remove from the freezer at least 10–15 minutes before serving.

Fruity adaptations

This ice-cream makes a wonderful base for fruity additions. The easiest way to add some fruit is to first make a simple compote. Add 120 g/1 cup soft fruit, such as strawberries or blueberries (fresh or frozen) to a small pan, along with 1 tablespoon brown sugar. Bring to a simmer for a few minutes over medium-high heat. Cook for 5–6 minutes until the fruit softens and forms a sticky jam. Set aside to cool in a bowl.

If you are making the ice-cream from scratch, add the blueberry or strawberry ripple part-way through churning or initial freezing. To adapt ice-cream already prepared, allow to soften at room temperature, then pour over the fruit sauce and create ripples in the ice-cream using a chopstick or skewer. Return to the freezer for a couple of hours.

European SUMMERS

TASTING THE WARMTH OF THE MEDITERRANEAN

EUROPEAN SUMMERS

As a child, I was lucky to enjoy many summers in Europe with my Francophile family. I've spent many weeks and months in the mountains and cities and on the beaches of this varied and beautiful country. Now my father lives in southern France with my step-mum. I may actually hold the country responsible for my inability to commit to a fully vegan diet. But even this cheese-loving vegetarian reaches a point where enough is enough, and I endeavour to seek out vegan food on my travels there. It's hard to believe that when I was a teenager, there was no word to explain 'vegetarian' in French, or that vegan was even a thing. They still look at you like you must be slightly crazy when you explain it to them. However, things in Europe are changing rapidly. Travel to the historic cities of Prague, Frankfurt or Berlin and you will find a completely different attitude towards vegan food today. From organic vegan burger joints and kebab shops to Chinese vegan fusion dining and hipster brunching, the options are growing incredibly fast.

I still don't find France (or Spain) the easiest place to dine out as a vegetarian, let alone vegan, but the local markets are unsurpassable for stunning produce from across the Med. Returning to the same place over and over again, essentially a home from home, gives me the chance to make local friends and travel to different regional markets. I was introduced to the wonderful markets in Antibes and Nice by local friends, and I especially love the Italian market in the border town of Ventimiglia. We take the coastal train from the small town where my dad lives, and usually return with more bags than we can carry or indeed eat. On more than one occasion I've had to pay for additional hold luggage so I can bring home even more goodies, mostly including several litres of olive oil, pistachios, macadamias, sun-dried vegetables, olives, pasta and all kinds of herbs and spices.

No matter where I travel in the world, I love to go to the local food markets. The sights and smells are sometimes overwhelming, but they are a great place to learn about local food. In Mediterranean Europe, I find the markets are a much more vegan-friendly place to eat. Whilst dining out can be dominated by dairy, the produce available in the markets is a vegan cook's dream. Some of these recipes were developed following a morning at a market, such as making pizzas with the biggest olives I've ever seen, local flour and the sweetest olive oil. Or recreating Asian flavours with something unexpected, like banana flower tempura with saffron aioli.

From left to right: French olive oil farm; Dolce Acqua, Italy; Garlic and chilli/chile vendor; view of Nice from Castle Hill; variety of olives on display at a French market.

I love having my own kitchen when I'm away. It can be the foodie saviour of the trip for me when in Europe, and it gives me a break from the same menu choices each night. I am often inspired after seeing a local dish that looked delicious but contained just a small amount of meat, so I had to miss out on trying it. Many of them can be prepared at home without the ubiquitous lardons; these little hammy surprises seem to be Europe's answer to fish sauce.

Our twin children took their very first steps in France. Along the banks of Lac d'Orient in the heart of the Champagne region, while we enjoyed some pink fizz in plastic camping wine glasses. Eating out in France could be tricky, but our camp-site cooking was always rather special. Tucking into pan-fried asparagus and mopping up garlicky olive oil with the best bread in the world – I doubt one could eat better in the neighbouring Michelin-starred restaurants. Camping in France and southern Europe is far more civilized than many non-campers would expect, and we could happily spend several weeks making our way around ancient volcanoes, gorges, forests and jaw-dropping coastlines. Europe has so much I still want to explore. Although I have now reached an age where I'd very much like to upgrade to a campervan.

There are also street food-inspired recipes here. What could be nicer than being able to hang around on a boulevard or beach with a handful of food? Drinking cold beer and eating socca (a kind of chickpea/garbanzo bean pancake) on the beach in Nice is one of my ultimate street food moments. No matter how many times I visit the city, I'm continually astounded by the architectural backdrop beside that bright azure water, and can sit for hours, people-watching on the promenade. It's easy to understand why so many artists took up residence along this coastline, along with so many of the rich and famous. But travellers should not be put off by its glamorous reputation. The South of France is easy to travel around on affordable public transport, boasting one of the greatest coastal train journeys in the world.

The recipes in this section are inspired by the flavours and food we've enjoyed on our summer travels around France, Spain and Italy, as well as extended stays with family. I can't remember ever returning from a trip without something new to try out in the kitchen at home. The recipes are about the flavours and the comforting nature of the dish, rather than adherence to authentic recipes. These recipes hold comforting memories of sunshine and holidays.

FRENCH ONION SOUP
with cashew cheese croutons

I'm a big soup lover. And after tomato, this is my other childhood favourite. Maybe it's because my dad was a Francophile and we often ate this as children, or maybe it's the lovely toppings. It joined a number of disappointing food moments when I found out there was a bone-based broth to the onions, but I came across vegetarian versions in the Savoie region of the Alps, where tourism has increased the veggie options available. You could use supermarket vegan mozzarella instead of the cashew 'cheese', if you like.

TO MAKE THE SOUP

3 tablespoons pomace or
    coconut oil
6–8 large Spanish onions,
    finely sliced
8 garlic cloves
½ teaspoon white pepper
½ teaspoon black pepper
1–2 teaspoons salt, to taste
1 teaspoon fresh thyme
    (or ½ teaspoon dried)
2 tablespoons plain/all-purpose
    flour
1.2 litres/5 cups water
350 ml/1½ cups vegan red wine
3 bay leaves
1 tablespoon good-quality
    vegetable stock powder/bouillon
    (such as Marigold)
1 teaspoon yeast extract
    (or 1 extra tablespoon stock
    powder/bouillon)

TO MAKE THE CASHEW CHEESE CROUTONS

120 g/1 cup cashews, soaked in
    water for 3 hours
300 ml/1¼ cups almond milk
2 tablespoons tapioca flour
4 tablespoons nutritional yeast
1 teaspoon garlic powder
½–1 teaspoon salt
½ baguette, cut at an angle into
    thick slices and toasted
handful of freshly snipped chives,
    to garnish (optional)

SERVES 4

Place a large heavy-bottomed pan over medium-high heat and add the oil and sliced onions. Sauté the onions for 20 minutes until they are nicely browned and softening. Stir well to avoid burning.

Add the garlic, white and black pepper, salt and thyme and cook for a further 5 minutes. Add the flour and cook for another 2 minutes. Add 250–500 ml/1–2 cups of the water and scrape the pan with a wooden spoon to ensure the onions are not sticking and the flour gets well mixed in with the liquid to form a thick paste.

Add the remaining water, wine, bay leaves, stock powder/bouillon and yeast extract and bring to the boil. Turn down the heat to the lowest setting and simmer for 40 minutes with the lid on. Stir about halfway through to ensure the onions are not sticking and add more water if necessary.

To make the cashew cheese, drain the soaked cashews and add to a blender with the almond milk, tapioca flour, nutritional yeast, garlic powder and salt. Blitz together to make a smooth paste, then pour into a small pan. Heat gently and stir well until the mixture thickens and becomes nice and gooey. Add more water as needed – if it cools and sets, just reheat and whisk back into a gooey mixture.

Check the seasoning in both the soup and the cashew cheese, and add more salt where needed.

Ladle the soup into deep bowls, top with a thick slice of toasted baguette and drizzle a spoonful or two of the cashew mixture. Add a sprinkle of freshly chopped chives, if you like, before serving.

DAD'S DINNER
Tempura courgette flowers

I love all kinds of tempura. I think food in batter is the second biggest crowd-pleaser on the UK street food circuit, after the ubiquitous burger. You can use the batter recipe here for all kinds of tender vegetables that will cook quickly, such as (bell) peppers or mushrooms. This is one of my dad's favourite dishes, and he always returns from his local market with a bagful of blossoms for me to cook when I'm visiting. He didn't really approve of my career change into food, abandoning a successful academic career (although there are days my weary back agrees with him). But then I cook him dishes like this, and he immediately forgets his disapproval.

12 courgette/zucchini blossoms (those with a big flower, small courgette/zucchini are best)
vegetable oil, for deep-frying

TO MAKE THE FILLING
150 g/5 oz. almond 'ricotta' (see page 15)
140 g/generous 1 cup frozen peas
¼ red onion
½ garlic clove
small handful of fresh mint
1 tablespoon freshly chopped coriander/cilantro
2 tablespoons soya or almond yogurt
¼–1 fresh red chilli/chile, to taste
freshly squeezed juice of ½ lime
½ teaspoon white pepper
½ teaspoon black pepper
1–2 teaspoons salt, to taste

TO MAKE THE BATTER
180 g/1¼ cups cornflour/cornstarch
250-ml/9-fl oz. bottle sparkling/soda water
1 teaspoon salt
½ teaspoon cumin powder

SERVES 4

First make the filling. Set aside the almond 'ricotta' and blend all the other ingredients together to a mousse-like paste. Fold the mixture into the almond 'ricotta'. Place in the fridge to set slightly.

Prepare the courgette/zucchini blossoms by checking the flowers for any resident creatures (a gentle shake outside should be enough to encourage them to find a new home). Carefully insert two fingers into the blossom and pinch off the inner stamen. You could also use a small paring knife. Don't worry if you get a little tear, as the batter will help hold it together. Trim the other end of the courgette/zucchini. If it is on the large side, slice down the centre to help it cook evenly.

Using a teaspoon, carefully fill the blossom with the pea mixture, using your finger to push the filling into the flower head. Do not overfill as you want to be able to twist and seal the end of the flower.

Heat the oil for deep-frying (approx. 6 cm/2¼ inches deep) over medium-high heat, until sizzling (test with a drop of batter, which should sizzle and not burn).

Whisk together the cornflour/cornstarch, sparkling/soda water, cumin powder and salt.

Working in batches, dip the courgettes/zucchini into the batter, then carefully place into the hot oil. Fry for 8–10 minutes until the batter is crispy and golden. Drain on paper towels, then keep warm in a low oven while you complete the batches. Serve immediately.

SOCCA *pizza*

Socca is a classic street food flatbread found around the Med (and known as farinata in Italy). Made with chickpea/garbanzo bean flour and olive oil, it's naturally gluten free. Around Nice, they tend to serve it quite simply, with lashings of olive oil and roasted garlic. It makes a fantastic base for pizza too, and much quicker to prepare than a traditional dough. This recipe includes a sprinkle of nigella seeds, but you can make the socca mixture plain or top it with whatever you like. The spinach topping makes a refreshing change from tomato pizza topping, and is perfect on its own or topped with a few shavings of vegan Italian-style hard cheese or some almond 'ricotta'.

TO MAKE THE TOPPING

1 tablespoon light olive oil
1 red onion, finely sliced
3 garlic cloves, crushed and chopped
200 g/7 oz. frozen spinach, defrosted and drained (or 500 g/1 lb. 2 oz. fresh)
¼ teaspoon fine salt
½ teaspoon black pepper

TO MAKE THE BASE

250 g/2¾ cups chickpea/garbanzo bean flour (gram flour)
400 ml/scant 1¾ cups water
½ teaspoon salt
1 scant teaspoon nigella seeds
1 tablespoon pomace or coconut oil

TO SERVE

150 g/5 oz. almond 'ricotta' (optional, see page 15)
chilli/chile oil or olive oil, for drizzling
1–2 teaspoons vegan Italian-style hard cheese (optional)

SERVES 6

Start by making the topping. Heat the olive oil in a small frying pan/skillet, add the sliced onion and sauté over medium heat for 8 minutes until softened and translucent. Add the garlic and cook for a further 3–4 minutes over high heat, so that the onion and garlic caramelize (but do not burn). Turn down the heat, add the spinach and mix well. Season with the salt and pepper and set aside.

In a large bowl, blend together the chickpea/garbanzo bean flour (gram flour) and water with a whisk to make a smooth pouring consistency. Season with the salt and add the nigella seeds.

Place a frying pan/skillet over a moderate heat and add the pomace or coconut oil. Ladle the batter into the pan/skillet, enough to cover the bottom of the pan and aiming for 5 mm–1 cm/¼–⅜ inch thickness. It's preferable to make them a little thinner if you are making garlic bread or flatbread for a wrap. Prepare all the bases, and set aside.

Preheat the grill/broiler to high.

Cover the socca base with the spinach mixture and a few small blobs of vegan 'ricotta'. Place under the hot grill/broiler for 5 minutes until a little charred at the edges. Serve immediately with a drizzle of chilli/chile oil (or olive oil if you prefer) and some vegan Italian-style hard cheese, if you like.

PANISSE *with truffled salt*

1 litre/4¼ cups water
285 g/generous 3 cups fine
    chickpea/garbanzo bean flour
    (gram flour)
600 ml/2½ cups pomace or
    vegetable oil, for deep-frying

TO MAKE THE TRUFFLED SALT
1–2 shavings of black truffle
1 tablespoon coarse rock salt

*2 baking pans, 1.25 cm/½ inch
    deep, oiled*

SERVES 4

Panisse are like chunky chickpea/garbanzo bean fries. You make them in a similar way to polenta, stirring liquid into the grain flour and mixing well to avoid any lumps. The texture you get will depend entirely on your stirring technique and the coarseness of the chickpea/garbanzo bean flour (gram flour). The street food sellers in the south of France tend to use fine gram flour, so the outside is super crispy and the inside is velvety and soft. Panisse reminds me of the Burmese food 'shan tofu', which is not tofu at all (tofu is made from soy beans) but is in fact made of fine gram flour that is set in the same way. Fried chunks of shan tofu or panisse can also be added to curries or used as a dipping vessel. Either way, they are a good source of vegan protein. You could bake them for a healthier snack, by simply brushing them with oil.

You can prepare truffle salt at any time by adding the truffle shavings, crumbled, to the coarse rock salt. The longer you leave this to infuse, the better the flavour will be. It can then be sprinkled any time over vegetables or pasta, or in this instance, panisse. For a quick version, finely mince the truffle shaving and place in bowl with the rock salt. Mix well, cover and set aside for half an hour.

Place the water in a pan over high heat and bring to the boil. When the water is almost boiling, start to whisk in the fine chickpea/garbanzo bean flour (gram flour). Keep whisking and adding until all the flour is combined and you have a thick, glossy paste. Cook gently for 5–6 minutes until the mixture is fully thickened.

Remove from the heat and pour the batter into the prepared baking pans. Leave to cool. Once set, slice into finger-sized batons.

Heat the oil for deep-frying to approx. 190°C (375°F) or until the oil is sizzling but not burning. Fry the batons in batches, turning carefully once or twice, for about 10–15 minutes. Ensure they are browned and golden all over, then drain on paper towels.

Serve them hot, with the truffled salt for sprinkling over, as a snack, or they make a delicious appetizer with an artichoke or mushroom dip.

Above: Vegetables for sale at Nice market.

BIG ASS *bagnat*

Whenever I'm near a beach or a ski slope in France, there always seems to be a pan-bagnat stall or café. This sandwich from Nice is made with the big, crusty sourdough roll known as pain de campagne, which is traditionally filled with the components of a Niçoise salad, layered high and then generously bathed in olive oil. The pan-bagnat stand near Beaulieu beach once made me a bagnat without the seafood and loaded up with veg, and it was such a delicious eating experience, I decided to recreate it at home with some extras. Their house tapenade has anchovies in it, but it's easy enough to make your own vegan tapenade. Try adding artichoke hearts for a delicious variation. The key to this sandwich is the quality of the ingredients used; an artisan or homemade sourdough roll or a crusty baguette or roll, fresh vegetables and a high-quality olive oil is a must.

1 aubergine/eggplant
1 red (bell) pepper
1 courgette/zucchini
½ fennel head
4 tablespoons extra-virgin olive oil, plus extra for drizzling
2 large artisan or homemade sourdough rolls (see page 75) or crusty baguettes or rolls
1 garlic clove, peeled and halved
1 red onion, finely sliced
handful of freshly chopped parsley
1–2 tablespoons balsamic vinegar
½ teaspoon rock salt
½ teaspoon ground black pepper

TO MAKE THE TAPENADE
200 g/scant 2 cups black olives, stoned/pitted, well rinsed
3 tablespoons capers, well rinsed
4 tablespoons olive oil
½ teaspoon salt

SERVES 2

Place a cast-iron griddle pan over high heat. Cut the aubergine/eggplant lengthways into thick 9-mm/⅜-inch slices. Cut the pepper in half and remove the core and seeds. Cut the courgette/zucchini into 6-mm/¼–inch slices. Cut the fennel into 3-mm/⅛-inch slices. Brush all the vegetables with the olive oil.

Lay the vegetables in the hot pan and griddle on all sides until nicely seared and well softened. Brush with more oil if needed. Season with the salt and pepper. Alternatively, you can roast the vegetables on a baking sheet in a hot oven. Set aside on paper towels to cool.

To prepare the tapenade, pulse all the ingredients in a blender to make a rough paste, or use a pestle and mortar to achieve a more traditional and slightly chunkier texture.

Cut the bread in half, and rub a halved garlic clove over it. Lightly toast the garlic-rubbed side and then cover with a generous layer of tapenade. Layer the griddled vegetables on top, and scatter with sliced red onion and chopped parsley. Then finish with a generous drizzle of extra-virgin olive oil and a little splash of balsamic. Place the lid of the roll on top, then wrap up tightly in foil or clingfilm/plastic wrap. Leave to chill for an hour or so, as the olive oil seeps through all the flavours and into the bread. Serve with a napkin!

PAIN DE CAMPAGNE *A simple sourdough*

**This everyday loaf or 'country bread' is simple to make
and a joy to eat, especially in the Big Ass Bagnats (see page 72).**

(see page 72)

TO MAKE THE SOURDOUGH STARTER
about 250 ml/1 cup tepid
    water
about 125 g/1 cup plain/
    all-purpose flour

DAY 1
30 g/1 oz. sourdough
    starter
100 g/3½ oz. strong
    organic white bread
    flour
100 ml/⅓ cup water

DAY 2
450 g/1 lb. strong white
    bread flour
400 ml/1¾ cups warm
    water
9 g/2 teaspoons salt

FOR DUSTING
50 g/6 tablespoons
    strong wholemeal/
    whole-wheat flour
50 g/6 tablespoons rice
    flour

*4 x 10–12-cm bread
proofing baskets for
rolls, or small bowls
baking sheet, lined with
baking parchment*

MAKES 4 ROLLS OR 1 LOAF

Sourdough starters take at least a week to prepare.
Mix 50 ml/3½ tablespoons tepid water with 25 g/
3 tablespoons flour, cover and leave somewhere
warm for 24 hours. Repeat this process every day
for 5–6 days, adding 50 ml/3½ tablespoons tepid
water and 25 g/3 tablespoons flour to the same bowl
and mixing each day. After 6–7 days, it should be
bubbling and smell yeasty like beer. The starter can
now be kept in the fridge until you need it (feeding
with a little more flour once a week).

To make the leaven, combine the Day 1
ingredients, mix well, cover and leave in a warm
place for 12 hours. The next day it should be frothy.

Combine the Day 2 ingredients (except the salt)
with 100 g/3½ oz. of leaven mixture from the day
before (put the other half in the fridge for another
loaf). Mix with your hands to form a sticky dough.
Cover the bowl with a kitchen towel and set aside in
a warm place for 40 minutes.

Use your hands to
combine the salt and
50 ml/3½ tablespoons warm
water with the dough. Mix well.
Cover and leave somewhere warm
for 30 minutes. Dip your hand in water, then
scoop down the side of dough. Lift the underside
and fold over the top. Turn the bowl slightly and
repeat the action. Rest the dough for 30 minutes,
then repeat the folding and resting process six times.

On a well-floured surface, cut the dough into four
equal pieces. Take each piece and fold the cut side up
and over the top of the dough, shaping into a round.
Cover with a kitchen towel and rest for 30 minutes.

In a small bowl mix together the dusting flours
and dust the proofing baskets with half the flour
mixture. Then dust the top of the dough rounds and
flip over so the dusted side is facing down. Pull out
each corner of the dough and fold over the top of
the round, repeating on each corner, as though you
are folding the sides of a piece of paper inwards.
Turn over the round so the folded side now faces
down, and shape each one into a round.

Transfer to floured proofing baskets or bowls,
folded-side now facing up. Cover with kitchen towels
and let rise for a few hours or overnight in the fridge.
If leaving overnight, allow the dough to sit at room
temp for 30–40 minutes before baking the next day.

Preheat the oven to 240°C (500°F) Gas 8.
Generously dust the top of the dough in baskets.

Turn out the rolls on the prepared baking sheet.
Use a baker's lame or razor blade to slice into the
tops of the rolls to allow for expansion. Bake for
10 minutes, then reduce the heat to 200°C (400°F)
Gas 6. Bake for 15–20 minutes more until the bottom
sounds hollow when tapped. Let cool on a wire rack.

CAMPFIRE RISOTTO
with asparagus, wild garlic and lemon

I adore asparagus. It's such a luxurious vegetable and keeps us on our toes in the UK with such a short season. In our early years together, Lee and I spent many months camping in Europe and with the extraordinary produce of warmer European climes, my campfire cooking rarely involved eating beans out of a can. Pan-fried vegetables from a local market with some garlic, olive oil and lemon or chilli flakes/hot red pepper flakes is always a comforting camping dish. I've never found chillies/chiles in France that contain the same spice we're used to enjoying in the UK, so I always carry some extra hot sauce on my travels. And a spice box in my kitchen camping box of course.

You can make this risotto with fresh asparagus, or you can use the cooked ones that come in a jar. I get the impression this is a little frowned upon in the UK, but in France and other parts of Europe there doesn't appear to be any snobbery about this. I love French-style, fat cooked asparagus, and the white ones are delicious chopped into a salad. Wild garlic/ramps can be a challenge to get hold of, but it can be found at local markets or on Spring foraging trips. Fresh baby spinach or chard can be added instead.

small bunch of new-season asparagus (approx. 9 stems), trimmed and cut into 2.5-cm/ 1-inch pieces
2 tablespoons olive oil
1 small white onion, chopped
1 celery stick, chopped
2 garlic cloves, crushed
200 g/generous 1 cup Arborio rice
½ glass of white wine (optional)
2 litres/8½ cups good-quality vegetable stock
25 ml/1½ tablespoons cashew or soy cream
120 g/4 oz. wild garlic/ramps, baby spinach or chard
1–2 teaspoons salt, to taste
½ teaspoon white pepper
½ teaspoon black pepper
freshly squeezed juice of ½ lemon
crusty baguette, to serve (optional)

SERVES 4–5

Prepare a bowl of iced water. In a large pan of boiling water, blanch the asparagus for 1–2 minutes, then place in the iced water and set aside. (When I'm camping, I just chop up the asparagus and throw it in the pan when the rice is half cooked.)

Heat 1 tablespoon of the olive oil in a deep frying pan/skillet and add the onion and celery. Sauté over low-medium heat until translucent and soft, about 10 minutes. Add the garlic and cook for another few minutes.

Add the rice and gently sauté until the rice is well coated. Add the wine and cook until it has completely reduced. Add a ladleful of stock, simmer and stir. Keep adding stock until the rice is soft and creamy. The rice should not be soggy, and it should still maintain a tiny bit of bite.

Add the asparagus, stir well and add a little more stock if needed. Add the cream and wild garlic/ramps and season well with the salt and pepper. It should be quite a loose consistency. Squeeze the lemon juice into the pan, stir well and serve immediately with crusty baguette.

BORDELAISE *suet pudding*

This dish was inspired by Crossroad Kitchen's porcini bordelaise, which has such eye-opening richness that it's truly hard to believe it is made with a vegan demi-glace. The secret to this dish is definitely in the roasted vegetable stock (see page 16), something I've been a fan of since my travels around Laos. The vegan demi-glace technique can be used on its own for making a super-rich wine gravy for other dishes, or even just on chips. Make larger quantities of the demi-glace (a day before is helpful) and freeze in portions to use later.

As a child growing up in the '70s and '80s, steamed suet puddings were comfort on a plate and my absolute favourite were the savoury ones from the chip shop. This Bordelaise-style sauce works sublimely with the crumbly pastry. Serve with lemon mash for a delicious contrast of flavours.

TO MAKE THE SUET PASTRY

250 g/scant 2 cups self-raising/self-rising flour
180 g/6½ oz. vegan suet
½ teaspoon salt
60 g/generous 1 cup fresh breadcrumbs, white or brown
½ teaspoon baking powder
125–150 ml/½–⅔ cup vegan milk, such as almond or soy

TO MAKE THE DEMI-GLACE

30 g/4 tablespoons plain/all-purpose flour
3 tablespoons olive or coconut oil
1 litre/4¼ cups roasted vegetable stock (see page 16)
2 bay leaves
1 teaspoon whole black peppercorns
1 teaspoon whole white peppercorns
4 sprigs of fresh rosemary
small handful of fresh thyme
2 tablespoons olive oil
1 teaspoon salt

TO MAKE THE FILLING

3 shallots, finely chopped
240 ml/1 cup red wine, such as Syrah, plus 3 tablespoons extra
1 bay leaf
3–4 sprigs of fresh thyme
2 tablespoons olive or coconut oil
280 g/10 oz. chestnut mushrooms, cleaned and quartered
30 g/1 oz. dried porcini mushrooms or other dried wild mushrooms, soaked in boiling water for 15 minutes
¼ teaspoon salt
½ teaspoon white pepper
small handful of freshly chopped parsley
1 sprig of rosemary, finely chopped
¼ teaspoon sugar

TO SERVE

olive oil mash (see page 185)
freshly squeezed juice of 1 lemon

1-litre/4-cup pudding basin, oiled

SERVES 4

In a large bowl, mix together the pastry ingredients, holding back at least 2 tablespoons of milk to ensure the dough is not too wet. Combine with your hands and knead a little to make a firm but supple dough. Flatten into a large disc and rest for 30–40 minutes.

For the demi-glace, add the flour to a medium heavy-bottomed pan and toast gently over medium heat for 1–2 minutes. Add the oil and cook for 10–15 minutes until the roux is lightly coloured and smells nutty. Slowly add the roasted stock, stirring constantly to make a smooth sauce. Add the remaining demi-glace ingredients, reduce the heat to low and simmer gently for about an hour until the sauce is reduced and coats the back of a spoon.

In a small pan, combine the shallots, wine, bay leaf and thyme for the filling. Bring to a simmer and cook for 10 minutes until reduced by half. Strain the wine mixture, then add 240 ml/1 cup of the demi-glace and mix well. The remaining demi-glace can be kept in the fridge for a few days or frozen for later use.

In a large frying pan/skillet or wok, add the oil, mushrooms and salt and pepper, and sauté for 6–8 minutes until the mushrooms begin to brown. Stir in the sauce to the pan, then add the remaining herbs and sugar, along with the extra 3 tablespoons of red wine. Bring to a simmer again, taste and add more salt and pepper if needed. Set aside.

Roll out the dough to 5 mm/¼ inch thick. Line the pudding basin, trimming the edges from the top and remoulding the trimmings to make a pastry lid. Add the filling, then place the pastry lid on top. Pinch the edges to seal, then cover with foil or baking parchment and tie with some string/twine if you like.

Place the basin in a large pan with enough water to come one-third of the way up the sides. Place a lid on the pan, bring to the boil and simmer on low for 3 hours. Do not let the pan boil dry.

Turn upside down onto a plate. Serve with olive oil mash, with the lemon juice mixed through.

BAKED AUBERGINE FRIES *with BBQ dip*

Courgette/zucchini fries were not just for holidays when we were kids. They were the exotic side dish we would all fight over at a birthday outing to our favourite Italian restaurant. Nowadays we just order more for the table. But they can have a tendency to be greasy and I prefer not to do too much deep-frying at home, mainly because of the washing up! These baked aubergine/eggplant fries make a great alternative, and can be served simply drizzled with a little balsamic vinegar or with this BBQ dip.

1 medium–large aubergine/eggplant

2–3 tablespoons potato flour or cornflour/cornstarch

2 flax 'eggs' (see page 12) or egg replacers

80 g/2 cups panko breadcrumbs

20 g/½ cup nutritional yeast

1 teaspoon rock salt

vegetable oil spray

TO MAKE THE BBQ SAUCE

500 ml/2 cups ketchup

60 ml/¼ cup cider vinegar

60 ml/¼ cup vegan Worcester sauce

50 g/¼ cup unrefined brown sugar

2 tablespoons molasses

2 tablespoons yellow mustard

1 tablespoon hot sauce, such as Tabasco or Dougie's (see page 38)

1 tablespoon 'magic dust' (see page 184)

½ teaspoon ground black pepper

baking sheet, lightly oiled

SERVES 2–3

Preheat the oven to 220°C (425°F) Gas 7.

Slice the aubergine/eggplant at an angle, into 2.5 cm/1 inch thick discs, then slice each disc into 2.5 cm/1 inch thick batons. Place the potato flour on a small plate. Place the flax 'egg' in one bowl and in a larger bowl, mix the breadcrumbs, nutritional yeast and salt.

Dip the aubergine/eggplant fries into the potato flour, then into the egg liquid and toss them in the breadcrumbs. Lay the breadcrumb-coated batons onto the lightly oiled baking sheet. Spray lightly with a little vegetable oil. Bake in the preheated oven for 20–25 minutes, turning once or twice to ensure they are golden and crispy all over.

While they are baking, add all the BBQ sauce ingredients to a small pan and place over medium-high heat. Bring to a simmer, and stir well until the sauce is thick and glossy. Set aside to cool. This sauce will keep for several weeks in the fridge if stored in a sterilized container.

Serve the aubergine/eggplant fries hot from the oven, with the BBQ sauce on the side for dipping. These are also nice served with a dip of soya yogurt mixed with garlic and herbs.

PAELLA *with harissa-roasted vegetables and paprika almonds*

Spain has long-standing tourism links to the UK. Whether or not this is what led to the tweaking and changing of their beloved paella, I don't know. The comedic scene from *Fawlty Towers* involving the hotel chef interfering with Manuel's beloved mama's recipe will always play on my mind when I make this recipe. Then Javi, one of my old staff and a young Spanish vegan, once told me he had tomatoes and bread for his birthday meal whilst out in Murcia, so I felt much less guilty about my recipe tampering.

You can substitute more tender vegetables in this dish, and omit the roasting, but there is something delicious about roasted vegetables. My children like to add vegan 'chorizo', but I suggest frying it a little first to colour and crisp it slightly.

scant ½ teaspoon saffron threads
250 ml/1 cup boiling water
1 aubergine/eggplant, cut into 2.5-cm/1-inch pieces
½ butternut squash, cut into 2.5-cm/1-inch pieces
½ cauliflower, cut into 2.5-cm/1-inch pieces
1 red (bell) pepper, cut into 2.5-cm/1-inch pieces
2 tablespoons harissa paste
1 tablespoon olive oil
3 tablespoons pomace or vegetable oil, plus an extra splash for the almonds
1 small red onion, finely chopped
4 garlic cloves, crushed
380 g/2 cups paella rice
2 bay leaves

1.2 litres/5 cups vegetable stock
1½ teaspoons sweet smoked paprika
1–2 teaspoons rock salt, to taste
2 fresh tomatoes, quartered
handful of whole soaked almonds, skins removed
½ teaspoon paprika
15–20 black olives, stoned/pitted and halved

TO SERVE
lemon wedges
crusty bread

2 baking sheets, oiled

SERVES 4–6

Soak the saffron in the boiling water for 10–15 minutes. Preheat the oven to 200°C (400°F) Gas 6.

Place the aubergine/eggplant, squash, cauliflower and red (bell) pepper in a bowl and add 1 tablespoon of the harissa paste and the olive oil. Use your hands to coat the vegetables in the spice paste. Place on the oiled baking sheets and roast for 20–25 minutes until soft and golden brown on the edges. Set aside.

Meanwhile, heat the pomace or vegetable oil in a paella pan or large frying pan/skillet and add the finely chopped onion. Sauté for a few minutes over medium heat until the onion softens, then add the garlic and cook for a further 5 minutes. Add the rice and ensure all the grains are well coated.

Add the bay leaves, stock, remaining harissa, sweet smoked paprika, saffron mixture, salt and tomatoes to the pan and mix well. Simmer over low heat for 15 minutes, until the rice is 85% cooked.

In a small pan, toast the almonds gently over medium heat in a tiny splash of oil. Add the paprika to coat the almonds, and toast for a few minutes until the aromas are released.

Add the roasted vegetables, olives and toasted almonds to the paella, and turn up the heat. Cook for 4–5 minutes. Do not stir to the bottom, to allow the bottom of the rice to crisp up slightly (but don't let it burn). Serve immediately in bowls with lemon wedges, and some crusty bread on the side.

SHIITAKE MUSHROOM *croquetas*

This vegan twist on a classic Spanish comfort dish will win over the most sceptical of diners, with the crispy exterior giving way to a rich, creamy centre. Croquetas traditionally have a thick béchamel filling, which is often spiked with Spain's favourite hammy surprise. You could use vegan 'lardons' or substitute other vegetables for the mushrooms if you like. Dried porcini make a good substitute for shiitake in this recipe.

TO MAKE THE FILLING

4 tablespoons olive oil

1 baby leek, finely sliced

2 bay leaves

½ teaspoon rock salt

4 tablespoons plain/all-purpose
   flour

500 ml/2 cups almond milk

3–4 dried shiitake mushrooms,
   soaked in boiling water

1 flax 'egg' (see page 12) or egg
   replacer

80 g/2 cups panko breadcrumbs

2 tablespoons nutritional yeast

½ teaspoon fine salt

½ teaspoon white pepper

olive oil, for deep-frying

1 tablespoon grated vegan Italian-
   style hard cheese, to serve
   (optional)

MAKES 10–12

To make the filling, heat 2 tablespoons of the olive oil in a frying pan/skillet over medium heat. Add the leek and sauté until softened. Add the bay leaves, salt and flour and stir well. Cook the flour mixture for about 3–4 minutes, and then slowly add the milk. Mix well to make a smooth paste. Keep cooking the flour mixture over gentle heat for about 10–15 minutes until well thickened, like mashed potato.

In a separate small pan, add the remaining 2 tablespoons olive oil and place over high heat. Chop the shiitake mushrooms into cubes and fry in the oil until slightly crisped. Set aside on paper towels.

Tip the filling mixture into a clean bowl, mix in the mushroom pieces and cover the surface with clingfilm/plastic wrap. Set aside to cool.

Put the flax 'egg' mixture in a small bowl and mix the panko breadcrumbs, nutritional yeast, salt and pepper in another small bowl.

When the mixture has cooled, use your hands to shape it into balls. Dip each ball into the 'egg' mixture then into the panko mixture. Set aside on a tray ready to fry.

Heat the olive oil for deep-frying in a deep pan over medium-high heat. When the oil is ready, it should just sizzle when you drop a little breadcrumb into the pan. Fry the croquetas, in batches, for about 6–8 minutes until golden brown all over. Drain on paper towels. Sprinkle with vegan Italian-style hard cheese, if you like. Serve at once, if they make it to the table!

SOFRITO-STYLE MEDITERRANEAN STEW
with saffron dumplings

This Mediterranean-inspired summery broth has lots of punchy flavours. Sofrito is a cooked flavour base often used for stews and soups in Spain, Portugal, Italy and Latin America, combining garlic, onions, tomatoes and smoky paprika. You can mix up the vegetables anyway you might prefer. Make sure you include all the fronds and leaves from the celery and fennel, as there is so much flavour in them.

250 ml/2 cups rapeseed or vegetable oil

1 white onion, finely sliced

3 garlic cloves, finely chopped

1 red chilli/chile, deseeded and finely chopped

3 celery sticks (with leaves), thickly sliced at an angle

2 heaped teaspoons smoked paprika

1 fennel head, halved lengthways and finely sliced

1 carrot, peeled and thinly sliced at an angle

1 small glass of white wine (preferably dry, optional)

small pinch of saffron threads

1½ 400-g/14-oz. cans chopped tomatoes (or 3–4 fresh ones)

400-g/14-oz. can chickpeas/garbanzo beans, rinsed and drained

1.5 litres/6¼ cups vegetable stock

2 or 3 (bell) peppers, red, yellow and/or orange, thickly sliced

1 courgette/zucchini, thickly sliced at an angle

2 teaspoons rock salt, or to taste

1 teaspoon white pepper, or to taste

freshly squeezed juice of ½ lemon

handful of fresh parsley, roughly torn

TO MAKE THE SAFFRON DUMPLINGS

300 g/2¼ cups plain/all-purpose flour

2½ teaspoons baking powder

1 teaspoon salt

120 g/4 oz. vegan suet or butter

½ teaspoon saffron threads, soaked in 100 ml/⅓ cup hot water for 20 minutes

SERVES 4

To prepare the dumplings, mix the flour, baking powder, salt and vegan suet in a large bowl. Add the saffron mixture, along with a little more water to make a very firm dough. Roll the dough into 8–10 balls. Set aside in the fridge.

Place a large, deep, heavy-bottomed pan over medium heat and add 2 tablespoons of the oil. Add the onion and sauté for 5–6 minutes.

Then add the garlic, chilli/chile and celery. Sauté for another 5–6 minutes, then add the paprika, fennel and carrot. Turn up the heat until the pan is sizzling, then add the white wine, if using. Stir well and then add the small pinch of saffron, along with the tomatoes, chickpeas/garbanzo beans and stock.

Bring to the boil and then reduce the heat. Add the (bell) peppers and courgette/zucchini, and stir well. Add more water if needed. Add the dumplings and simmer for 20–30 minutes, until the fennel and celery are tender and the dumplings are fluffy and have almost doubled in size.

Season with the rock salt and white pepper to taste. Just before serving, add the lemon juice and scatter with some fresh parsley on top.

ARTICHOKE TORTA
with saffron mayonnaise

Ventimiglia market in north-west Italy is one of my favourite food markets, and judging by the packed trains arriving from both sides of the border on Friday's big market day, I'm not the only one to fall for this emporium of Mediterranean produce. Every corner you turn, there are busy cafés spilling out onto the bustling streets, ready to fuel your shopping with fearsomely strong coffee. And with a torta stand on every other corner, these Italian-style pies are also hard to resist.

Lighter than most British pies, the flaky, crispy pastry with a rich and savoury filling, is served across Italy, and usually packed with eggs and butter. Try serving these with polenta chips and saffron aioli for a fresh take on pie and chips.

450 g/1 lb. artichoke hearts (approx. 5 fresh artichokes or 1½ small jars)

2 tablespoons pomace or vegetable oil

2 banana shallots, finely chopped

2 garlic cloves, crushed and chopped

100 g/3½ oz. barely cooked white rice

2 tablespoons fine chickpea/garbanzo bean flour (gram flour)

1–2 teaspoons salt, to taste

2 tablespoons nutritional yeast

8 filo/phyllo pastry sheets

TO MAKE THE SAFFRON MAYONNAISE
¼ teaspoon saffron threads, soaked for 10 minutes in 2 tablespoons boiling water

5 generous tablespoons vegan mayonnaise (see page 12)

4 small tart pans or shallow pie pans (7.5 cm/3 inch), or 1 large shallow pie pan (25 cm/10 inch), lightly oiled

SERVES 4

First slice the fresh artichoke hearts. If using jarred artichokes, rinse with warm water, drain and dry well before slicing.

Preheat the oven to 170°C (340°F) Gas 4.

Heat ½ tablespoon of the oil in a small frying pan/skillet and sauté the shallots for 6–7 minutes until soft and translucent. Add the garlic and cook for another 2 minutes. Set aside.

Add the prepared artichoke hearts to the shallot and garlic mixture, along with the cooked rice. In a small bowl, mix together the fine chickpea/garbanzo bean flour (gram flour) with 4–6 tablespoons of water, or enough to make a thick but pourable paste. Add the paste to the artichoke mixture, along with the salt and nutritional yeast. Mix well to ensure all the ingredients are well combined.

If using individual pans, layer two sheets of filo/phyllo pastry into the pan, offsetting the squares to make a star shape and ensuring the pastry is snugly pushed into the corners. If using a large pie pan, layer your filo/phyllo sheets one at a time, offsetting each sheet to ensure there is at least a double layer of pastry all the way around the pan.

Fill the pastry with the artichoke mixture, until level with the top edge of the pan, then fold and twist the pastry across the top, so the filling is covered and the pie is sealed.

Lightly brush the top of the pastry with the remaining oil. Place the pies onto a baking sheet and bake in the preheated oven for about 30–35 minutes until the pastry is golden brown (if baking one large pie, cook for a further 15 minutes).

Strain the saffron water to remove the threads, then whisk the saffron water into the vegan mayonnaise, adding slowly and whisking all the time. Serve the warm pies with a generous spoonful of the saffron mayonnaise. It is also nice with polenta chips and a chopped salad.

ROASTED AUBERGINE LASAGNE *with Puy lentils*

We love a good vegetarian lasagne in our house. I don't think you can beat a homemade one. I think the dish benefits from being left overnight and baked the following day, but a few hours in the fridge will do the job if pushed for time. The lentils can be substituted for vegan 'mince' and the aubergines/eggplant for courgettes/zucchini.

TO MAKE THE LENTIL MIXTURE
2 tablespoons olive oil
1 large onion, diced
4 garlic cloves, crushed
250 g/generous 1¼ cups Puy lentils
750 ml/3¼ cups vegetable stock,
    plus extra if needed
12 large tomatoes
1 carrot, diced
1 red (bell) pepper
1 celery stick, diced
2 tablespoons dark soy sauce
1 bay leaf
handful of fresh marjoram
handful of fresh thyme
2 tablespoons tomato purée/paste
½ teaspoon salt, or to taste
½ teaspoon black pepper, or to taste

TO MAKE THE AUBERGINE/EGGPLANT LAYER
2 aubergines/eggplants
2 tablespoons olive oil
sea salt and black pepper

TO MAKE THE 'BÉCHAMEL'
2 tablespoons olive oil
½ teaspoon salt, or to taste
½ teaspoon white pepper,
    or to taste
2 tablespoons plain/all-purpose
    flour
400 ml/scant 1¾ cups almond
    or soy milk
1 bay leaf
½ teaspoon mustard powder

TO ASSEMBLE
1 packet of egg-free lasagne sheets
120 g/4 oz. grated vegan Italian-
    style hard cheese
sea salt and black pepper, to taste

Start with the lentil mixture. Heat 1 tablespoon of the olive oil in a pan and sauté half of the onion and one clove of crushed garlic until softened. Add the Puy lentils and sauté for a further minute, then add the stock and simmer until the lentils are fully cooked and soft. Add further stock as needed; you are aiming for the lentils to absorb most of the liquid without leaving too much broth.

Preheat the oven to 210°C (410°F) Gas 6.

Remove the hard cores from the tomatoes. Place them whole on a baking sheet, along with the 3 remaining crushed garlic cloves and cook in the oven until well roasted and almost starting to blacken. Blitz with a hand blender and set aside.

To make the aubergine/eggplant layer, remove the ends of the aubergines/eggplants. Slice them lengthways into 1.5 cm/½ inch thick slices. Place on a baking sheet, drizzle with the olive oil and season. Roast on high heat until golden brown and soft. Set aside.

Reduce the oven to 190°C (375°F) Gas 5.

Back to the lentil mixture. Heat the remaining 1 tablespoon olive oil in a pan and sauté the remaining half of onion, along with the carrot, red (bell) pepper and celery, then add the cooked lentils, soy sauce, bay leaf, the fresh marjoram and thyme. Add the blended tomatoes and the tomato purée/paste. Bring to the boil and simmer for 10 minutes. Add the salt and pepper, then adjust the seasoning according to taste.

To make the 'béchamel', heat the olive oil in small, deep pan, add the salt, white pepper and flour, and cook to make a roux. Gently cook the paste for 2–3 minutes. Slowly add the milk, whisking all the time, until it reaches a creamy sauce consistency. Add the bay leaf and the mustard powder, and simmer for 2–3 minutes. Check the seasoning.

Layer some 'béchamel' sauce in the bottom of a large, deep baking dish and cover with lasagne sheets. Add half the lentil and tomato mixture, followed by a layer of aubergine/eggplant, using all the slices and overlapping them to create a thick layer. Add the remaining lentil mixture, a layer of lasagne sheets and top with the 'béchamel'. Sprinkle with vegan cheese, salt and pepper.

Bake for 30–40 minutes until bubbling and the top is golden brown.

SERVES 6–8

MOROCCAN-STYLE VEGETABLE CLAYPOT
with quinoa

1–2 tablespoons pomace or olive oil

1–2 white onions roughly chopped

4 garlic cloves, crushed

2 teaspoons sumac

1 teaspoon hot paprika or mild chilli/chili powder

300 g/10½ oz. frozen vegan Quorn pieces (optional)

1 large aubergine/eggplant, cut into 2.5-cm/1-inch pieces

1 yellow (bell) pepper, cut into strips

½ cauliflower, cut into florets

400-g/14-oz. can chickpeas/garbanzo beans, rinsed and drained

2 tablespoons tomato purée/paste

2 400-g/14-oz. cans chopped tomatoes

2 bay leaves

large handful of fresh thyme

1 tablespoon agave syrup

1 tablespoon pomegranate molasses

1.5 litres/6¼ cups vegetable stock

2 teaspoons cumin seeds, toasted

2–3 preserved lemons, quartered

115 g/1 cup green olives, stoned/pitted

1–2 teaspoons salt, to taste

200 g/generous 1 cup quinoa, cooked for 10 minutes in 285 ml/1¼ cups vegetable stock, then left to stand for 5 minutes

handful of freshly chopped herbs, such as marjoram, parsley or coriander/cilantro, to serve

SERVES 5–6

For those of you unfamiliar with quinoa, it is a type of grain that originated in South America. The Incas believed the crop was sacred, and this is hardly surprising given it kicks the nutritional backside of most other cereals and grains, containing essential amino acids as well as calcium and iron. But unfortunately, quinoa is not like rice, with its sexy, subtle flavours. It's fairly bland, even when it's showing off its different colours. Making the sauce sing with flavour is the key to making the quinoa join in the chorus. The recipe looks like a lot of ingredients, but it is very much a 'chuck it all in a pot' type of dish. You could also substitute any vegetables really, such as carrots, sweet potato or courgettes/zucchini.

Heat the oil in a deep, heavy-bottomed pan and soften the onions until translucent. Add the garlic, sumac, paprika and Quorn pieces (if using). Cook for a further 1–2 minutes, then add all the remaining ingredients, except the quinoa. Ensure there is plenty of liquid in the pan, as this will be absorbed by the quinoa later. Bring to a simmer and cook, covered, over very low heat for 50–60 minutes.

Stir the ingredients well, then layer the soaked quinoa over the top. Replace the lid and leave to stand for 5 minutes. Sprinkle with the freshly chopped herbs just before serving. This is nice served with warm crusty bread or a green salad.

SWEETCORN COBS
with salted chilli olive oil

Everyone assumes that only butter makes the best buttery taste but it is simply not true. A good-quality virgin olive oil is the perfect addition to whip up the creamiest mash, or for smothering some plump, seasonal vegetables. It is really easy to find good-quality olive oil these days and the flavour profiles can be sublime. I make this with a buttery-tasting Sicilian blend, together with a good pinch or two of Himalayan rock salt. I promise you won't miss the butter.

140 ml/scant ⅔ cup good-quality
    olive oil (I use Sicilian or Calabrian)
½ tablespoon Himalayan rock salt
1–2 teaspoons dried chilli flakes/hot
    red pepper flakes
4 corn cobs, trimmed and halved

SERVES 4

In a large bowl, mix together the olive oil, salt and chilli flakes/hot red pepper flakes and set aside for 20–30 minutes.

Preheat the oven to 220°C (425°F) Gas 7.

Place a corn cob on a large foil square, spoon over some of the chilli oil mix and then wrap well in the foil. Repeat for each of the cobs and reserve the bowl with the remaining oil. Place the cobs on a baking sheet in the preheated oven and roast for 45–50 minutes until the corn is cooked.

Remove the cobs from the foil and tip them back into the large bowl with the remaining spicy oil. Toss them around so that they are well coated, then serve immediately.

PEAR AND FRANGIPANE *tart*

Frangipane tarts are one of my go-to vegan desserts, because they don't have to be made with eggs. It feels indulgent and pairs so well with different fruits – the combinations are fairly endless and you can adapt to the different seasons. I sometimes make this tart with greengages, a highly regarded sweet plum, but they're not easy to find in the UK, whereas pears are readily available everywhere.

350 g/12 oz. vegan pastry
   (see page 16)
4 large pears
freshly squeezed lemon juice
150 g/5½ oz. vegan margarine or
   coconut butter, cut into pieces
150 g/¾ cup granulated sugar
180 g/1¾ cups ground almonds
50 g/6 tablespoons plain/
   all-purpose flour
½ teaspoon ground cinnamon
small pinch of salt
160 ml/⅔ cup plain almond milk
½ vanilla pod/bean, halved
   lengthways and seeds scraped
   (or 2 teaspoons pure vanilla
   extract)
½ teaspoon almond extract
60 g/scant 3 tablespoons apricot
   jam/jelly
icing/confectioners' sugar,
   for dusting
vegan vanilla ice-cream or almond
   cream, to serve

*large 20–24-cm/8–10-inch tart
   pan or four 8–10-cm/3–4-inch
   individual tart pans, greased with
   vegan margarine or butter*
baking beans

SERVES 4

Preheat the oven to 160°C (325°F) Gas 3.

Prepare the pastry base, by rolling out the pastry on a well-floured surface to 3–4 mm/⅛ inch thickness. Line the greased tart pan(s) with the shortcrust pastry, ensuring the pastry is pushed into the corners or fluted edge and allowing the pastry to overhang the top edge of the pan. Cover the pastry with baking parchment, and then add the baking beans to cover the tart base. If you have time, rest this pastry case in the fridge for 20 minutes.

Bake in the preheated oven for 25–30 minutes until the pastry is almost cooked with little colour. Take the tart base out of the oven and remove the beans and paper. Place back in the oven, uncovered, for 10 minutes. Remove and set aside ready to fill.

Peel the pears, slice in half and remove the cores. Set aside in a bowl of lemon water to stop them browning.

In a food processor, blitz together the margarine, sugar, ground almonds, flour, ground cinnamon and salt. Continue to pulse and then slowly pour in the almond milk, along with vanilla seeds (or extract if using) and almond extract. Mix to form a thick batter. Spread the almond mixture into the tart case. Slice each pear half with crossways cuts to create a fan. Gently press each pear fan into the mixture.

In a small pan, melt the jam for a few minutes over medium heat, stirring often. Alternatively melt in a microwave for a minute or two. It should be liquid enough to brush on top of the pie.

Bake the tart in the preheated oven for 30–40 minutes until the top is golden brown, then move the tart onto a cooling rack and cool for 20 minutes. Brush the top of the tart and pears with the melted jam. Leave the tart to cool for another hour or so. Dust with icing/confectioners' sugar and serve with a scoop of vanilla ice-cream or some almond cream.

PANNA COTTA *with candied kumquats*

My step-mum is queen of the oranges in our family, and she makes a range of marmalades and jams with the glut of citrus fruit from their Mediterranean garden. Some of you may be familiar with my Marmalade Tofu recipe in *Vegan Street Food*. That recipe is even more delicious with my step-mum's kumquat marmalade. Last summer, I made candied kumquats as they are the perfect size and shape for a dessert, and will keep for several months.

    The panna cotta is a great summery pudding – light and creamy and satisfying all at the same time. This makes a perfect ending to any dinner party. Mainly because it's already prepared and no-one wants to be in the kitchen at this point in the evening. My MasterChef buddy Sara often serves perfectly formed sable biscuits alongside this Italian classic. But Oreos also work brilliantly too!

FOR THE CANDIED KUMQUATS

250 ml/1 cup water
300 g/1½ cups granulated sugar
½ vanilla pod/bean, halved
lengthways and seeds scraped
500 g/1 lb. 2 oz. kumquats

FOR THE PANNA COTTA

2 tablespoons cornflour/cornstarch
700 ml/scant 3 cups soy milk
80 g/5½ tablespoons caster/
granulated sugar
9 g/1 tablespoon agar agar
250 ml/1 cup orange juice

6–7 small panna cotta moulds
or cups

MAKES 6–7

To make the candied kumquats, in a small saucepan, heat the water, sugar, vanilla seeds and the scraped pod/bean, and bring to a simmer. Add the kumquats, reduce the heat and simmer for 15–20 minutes until the kumquats are tender and soft, and the syrup is thick enough to coat a spoon. Set aside.

For the panna cotta, dissolve the cornflour/cornstarch in 2–3 tablespoons of the milk, and set aside. Mix the remaining milk with the sugar, agar agar and orange juice in a small pan. Bring to a simmer, and cook for 6 minutes. Add the cornflour/cornstarch mixture and cook for a further 3–4 minutes.

Strain through a fine sieve/strainer into 6 or 7 small cups or moulds. Leave to cool for 15 minutes, then set aside in the fridge for at least an hour.

Just before serving, spoon two or three of the candied kumquats on top of the dessert, and drizzle some of the leftover sauce over the top.

Asian
COMFORT

WARMING SPICES AND INTOXICATING AROMAS

ASIAN COMFORT

My love for Asian food has not dwindled. I think a lot of Asian food has the comfort factor, especially the fragrant noodle broths and spicy curries. There's no shortage of tasty fried snacks either, which always make a lovely treat or accompaniment.

The India section of my previous book was packed with delicious recipes, so some of my favourite comfort dishes from the subcontinent are included here. Some of these dishes are very much about the comforting feeling of home, not just our travels. Indian food, Punjabi and Gujurati especially, have played a large part in my culinary experiences in Manchester. The city is blessed with fabulous Indian eateries, from local dhabas to Mumbai-style cafés and dining rooms. Even better than this, I sometimes get little food packages from my friend Seema, and her mum Mrs G; simply because she knows how much I love her Gujurati food.

Manchester is also home to the biggest Chinatown outside London, and the rather Anglicized but crowd-pleasing Chinese restaurants were where we often dined out as children. Many Brits associate this style of food with comfort food; the weekend takeaway treat and that ultimately familiar combination of sweet and salty and sour and hot.

I've included some memorable Nepali-inspired dishes here, too. I say inspired, because in Nepal, you often eat what is abundant at that time of year, and these dishes reflect that approach. Their love of eating easy-growing leafy greens like nettles and spinach is easy to become addicted to. Nepal holds a very special place in our hearts, with some mixed emotions of love and awe for the mountain landscape, tinged with sadness for the losses we've experienced here. We spent several months with local friends in this incredible place during 2009, and while we introduced Biz and Parin to the wonders of creamy mashed potato, they acquainted us with nettle curry. Parin and I met through my old area of work in Harm Reduction, and she works tirelessly as a director for the charity Dristi Nepal, supporting female drug users. Following the

From left to right: Tiffin carrier, India; chaat seller, India; dragon bell at a Hindu temple; snacks being arranged by street food seller, Cambodia; Mekong sunset, Cambodia.

devastating earthquake in 2015, Dristi were able to utilize their networks on the ground to get aid and help directly to people who needed it.

Another country from our 'gap year' that I simply couldn't squeeze into the last book was Cambodia. It's difficult not to fall in love with this beautiful country, with a history that almost breaks your heart. We spent our days exploring atmospheric, jungle-encased temples, making friends with welcoming locals, searching for elusive dolphins and sampling delicious and fragrant food. Sharing stories with my bus seat companion en route to Phnom Penh was an education, although I kindly declined his offer of some deep-fried cockroaches. It can be hard for us to understand why people eat such things, but when hunger dominated people's lives during the war-torn famines, everything became edible for survival, and some remain as delicacies. Travelling overland opens your eyes to the extent of unexploded ordnance and the resulting limb loss, highlighting just how dangerous it is to wander off the beaten path here.

One of our favourite towns was Kratie (pronounced kra-chay), on the wide-rolling banks of the Mekong, with gorgeous Colonial French-era architecture. Like many towns in previous colonial countries, it was once highly developed then devastated by war. It's also home to the Irrawaddy dolphin. These serene fellows don't leap about like their bottle-nosed and spinner cousins. As we bobbed about in our boat, their backs gracefully arched out of the water and every now and then you got to peek at their round faces. We watched the blissful Mekong sunset while eating jahk chien, crispy nuggets of banana and yam fried in a coconut and sesame batter.

This section is firmly back on the street food track, as it's simply how we like to eat when we're in Asia. I love the tapas-like plates of street food and big bowls of noodles to share. Like my first book, Vegan Street Food, some of these dishes are authentically inspired recipes, whereas other dishes are fusion recreations. There's plenty of adaptability in the recipes to make the best of seasonal produce, too.

PUNJABI PIE *and gravy*

Dal-topped samosas are my husband's favourite lunch. He always asks for this in our favourite thali cafe in Manchester. Turns out it is the owner Fred's favourite lunch, too. It's like a Punjabi take on pie and gravy! A rather fitting dish for our northern city I think. The samosa is quite traditional with potato and pea, but you can mix it up with whatever vegetables you like. The 'gravy' is a buttery-tasting dhaba-style dal, served at roadside stops across Nepal, India and Pakistan, and on Fred's Tuesday special. You can substitute the spice mix here with 2 teaspoons of garam masala, if you like. Serve with a dollop of hot pickle on the side (such as the chilli/chili pickle on page 17).

TO MAKE THE DAL

180 g/1 cup mixed dal/lentils (or you can substitute any mix of red lentils, split urad dal or mung beans, all split, preferably with husk on), soaked in water for at least an hour

1 teaspoon ground turmeric

1–2 tablespoons vegetable oil

1 teaspoon cumin seeds

1 stick of cinnamon

3 cloves

2 green cardamoms

2 bay leaves

1 onion, diced

1.5-cm/½-inch thumb of ginger, chopped

8 garlic cloves, crushed and chopped

1–2 fresh green chillies/chiles, to taste

1–2 dried red chillies/chiles, to taste

1 tablespoon kasuri methi (dried fenugreek leaves)

1 large tomato, chopped

½–1 teaspoon chilli/chili powder

1 teaspoon ground coriander

½ teaspoon garam masala

pinch of asafoetida (hing, optional)

1 litre/4¼ cups water

1–2 teaspoon rock salt, to taste

TO MAKE THE PASTRY

240 g/1¾ cups plain/all-purpose flour

1 teaspoon ajwain (carom) seeds

4 tablespoons vegetable oil

1 teaspoon sea salt

6 tablespoons water

TO MAKE THE SAMOSA FILLING

1 teaspoon cumin seeds

1 clove

4 black peppercorns

2 green cardamoms

½ teaspoon fennel seeds

1 teaspoon coriander seeds

1 tablespoon coconut or vegetable oil

5–7.5-cm/2–3-inch thumb of ginger, finely chopped

1–2 green chillies/chiles, to taste, finely chopped

1 teaspoon mild chilli/chili powder

1 teaspoon amchoor (green mango powder)

pinch of asafoetida (hing)

2 large potatoes, peeled and cut into 1-cm/⅜-inch cubes, parboiled

140 g/generous 1 cup frozen peas

½ teaspoon salt, to taste

1 litre/4¼ cups vegetable oil, for deep-frying

TO SERVE

handful of freshly chopped coriander/cilantro

finely chopped green chilies/chiles (optional)

SERVES 4–6

Start with the dal. Rinse the mixed dal/lentils and add to a large pan of water along with ½ teaspoon of the ground turmeric. Ensure there is at least double the amount of water to mixed dal/lentils, then bring to the boil and simmer for 1 hour 30 minutes over low heat, until the mix dal/lentils are completely softened. Drain any excess water (it doesn't matter if there's a little left in the pan), then lightly mash and set aside.

In another pan or wok, heat the vegetable oil and add the cumin seeds, stick of cinnamon, cloves, green cardamoms and bay leaves. Sauté until they crackle, then add the diced onion. Cook over low-medium heat for 10–15 minutes until the onion is translucent and lightly golden.

Add the ginger, garlic, green chillies/chiles and dried red chillies/chiles. Sauté for another 3–4 minutes, then add the kasuri methi, tomato, chilli/chili powder, ground coriander, garam masala, asafoetida (if using) and the remaining ½ teaspoon turmeric. Add the water and the cooked mixed dal/lentils, then stir well. Bring to a simmer for about 30 minutes, stirring occasionally to ensure that it doesn't stick to the pan and burn. Add the salt to taste.

To make the samosas, prepare the pastry by mixing together the flour, ajwain seeds, oil and salt. Rub together to create a crumb consistency.

Add the water gradually, kneading together until you get a soft dough. Cover with a damp kitchen towel and leave to rest for 30 minutes.

Set aside ½ teaspoon of whole cumin seeds to use in the filling, then toast the rest of the whole spices for the samosa in a pan and then grind them to a fine powder (I use a coffee grinder, or you can use a pestle and mortar).

Heat the oil in a large frying pan/skillet or wok and add the ginger and green chilli/chile. Cook gently for about 2–3 minutes, then add the remaining ½ teaspoon whole cumin seeds, and cook for another 1–2 minutes until they start to crackle.

Add the freshly ground spice mix (or use 2 teaspoons garam masala) and then the chilli/chili powder, amchoor, asafoetida and potato cubes. Mix well and cook gently for 3–4 minutes.

Remove from the heat and add the peas and salt. Check the seasoning and adjust to taste. Mix well and set aside to cool.

Knead the dough and divide into 6–8 equal balls. Lightly dust the work surface with flour and roll out the balls into large discs.

Cut each circle of pastry in half down the middle and take one half of the pastry into your hand. Brush some water down the straight edge and bring together those edges, like a cone, and seal them well.

Fill the cone of pastry with about a tablespoonful of filling, then dampen the edge and seal closed by pinching the top edges together. Repeat with the remaining dough to make 12–16 samosas (depending on how big you want to make them).

For a healthier option, the samosas can also be baked in a moderate oven for 30–40 minutes (180°C (350°F) Gas 4). Just brush them lightly with some oil prior to baking.

To fry the samosas, heat the vegetable oil for deep-frying in a deep pan. Drop a cube of bread into the oil to check that the oil is hot enough; it should sizzle immediately and rise to the surface.

Gently fry your samosas, in batches, for about 8 minutes, turning halfway through. Drain the samosas on paper towels, then keep them warm in a low oven while you cook the remaining batches. Alternatively, allow them to cool and then reheat later. They will keep in the fridge for several days.

To serve, place one or two samosas on a plate, and pour a ladle or two of dal over the top. Scatter with fresh coriander/cilantro and chopped green chillies/chiles, if you like.

PAV BHAJI
Vegetable mash with turmeric roll

We did an extraordinary amount of eating in Mumbai, repeatedly drawn into the cafés by the wafts of delicious food. Mumbai's southern tip is a great area to discover on foot, and we were always well fuelled by regular café stops and the street food wallahs along Chaupati. This street food haven is one of the great snacking spots of the world. Pav Bhaji is a Mumbai fave, popular across the state of Maharashtra and on trendy Indian restaurant menus across the UK.

The 'pav' or 'pao', an Indo-Portugeuse roll, is sometimes served with a spiced vegetable patty (like a spicy potato burger, called 'vada pav') or with a moreish and comforting bowl of spicy vegetable mash (bhaji). The dish normally includes large quantities of butter so this version is a little healthier, but it's still altogether comforting. You can buy some readymade rolls, if you don't fancy baking, but this recipe makes a good soft Bombay-style pav.

3 waxy potatoes, peeled and diced into 1-cm/⅜-inch pieces

¼ cauliflower, cut into small florets

2 carrots, peeled and diced into 1-cm/⅜-inch pieces

3–6 tablespoons coconut or vegetable oil, to taste

1 teaspoon cumin seeds

1 large onion, finely chopped

4 garlic cloves, crushed and chopped (or 1 teaspoon garlic paste)

6.5-cm/2½-inch thumb of ginger, finely chopped (or 1 teaspoon ginger paste)

1–2 fresh green chillies/chiles, to taste, finely chopped

3 large tomatoes, core removed, diced

1 green (bell) pepper, finely chopped

2 tablespoons homemade pav bhaji masala powder (see right) or 3 tablespoons readymade pav bhaji masala powder or 3 tablespoons garam masala plus 1 tablespoon amchoor (green mango powder)

1 teaspoon ground turmeric

1 teaspoon chilli/chili powder

pinch of garam masala

160 g/1¼ cups frozen peas (or dried peas, soaked overnight)

100 g/3½ oz. green beans, chopped into 1-cm/⅜-inch pieces

TO MAKE THE PAV BHAJI POWDER

25 g/⅞ oz. cumin seeds

15 g/½ oz. fennel seeds

11 g/⅓ oz. coriander seeds

3 g/⅛ oz. nutmeg (mace)

6 g/¼ oz. cloves

10 g/⅓ oz. black peppercorns

2 black cardamoms

3 star anise

5 g/⅙ oz. nutmeg

4 g/scant ⅙ oz. cinnamon sticks

4 whole dried red chillies/chiles

2 tablespoons amchoor (green mango powder)

1 tablespoon ground ginger

2 teaspoons black salt or regular salt

1 teaspoon ground turmeric

TO MAKE THE TURMERIC PAVS

2 teaspoons active dry yeast

200 ml/scant 1 cup lukewarm water

1¼ teaspoons sugar

400 g/3 cups plain/all-purpose flour

1 teaspoon ground turmeric

1 teaspoon salt

2 tablespoons olive oil

2 tablespoons vegan milk, for brushing

nigella seeds, for sprinkling (optional)

TO SERVE

1 tablespoon vegan butter or olive oil

handful of fresh coriander/cilantro

1 small red onion, finely chopped

1 lemon or lime, cut into wedges

SERVES 4–6

To make the pav bhaji powder, use a digital scale and weigh out the spices, then grind the whole spices to a powder, mix together and sieve/strain. Store in an airtight container.

Half-fill a large pan with water and place over high heat. Add the prepared potatoes, cauliflower and carrots, and boil for 5 minutes until the potato is soft. Drain, lightly mash and set aside. Do not over-mash; it should remain very lumpy.

In a small pan, melt the coconut or vegetable oil over high heat, then add the cumin seeds followed by the chopped onion. Sauté for 5 minutes, then add the garlic and ginger, and cook for a further few minutes. Add the chillies/chiles, tomatoes, green (bell) pepper, pav bhaji powder, turmeric, chilli/chili powder and garam masala. Mix well and cook over low heat for about 15 minutes, until everything is well cooked and soft, and you can see the oil is released. Add the mashed vegetables, peas and green beans, then combine well. Add more water to achieve the consistency of a soupy stew, and season with salt as needed. Mash the curry a little more and allow to simmer over low heat for 10–15 minutes more. Adjust the seasoning to taste, and add more salt, pav bhaji powder and chilli/chili powder if needed.

To make the pavs, mix the yeast, lukewarm water and ¼ teaspoon of the sugar together with 1 tablespoon of the flour in a large bowl. Mix well to make a smooth batter, cover and set aside for 30–40 minutes, until frothy and risen. Add the remaining flour along with the turmeric, salt, remaining sugar and oil. Knead well for 10 minutes to make a soft pliable dough. Cover the dough with oil and set aside in a bowl for about 1 hour, until it has doubled in size.

Punch down and knead slightly, then shape into 10 balls. Place the well-oiled balls onto a baking tray, and leave to rise again for about 1 hour.

Preheat the oven to 200°C (400°F) Gas 6.

Brush the pavs with some vegan milk (I like to sprinkle a few nigella seeds on the top, too) and bake in the oven for 25–30 minutes. Tap the bottom of the roll to check for a hollow sound and ensure the rolls are cooked through. Cool the rolls on a wire rack.

To serve, heat the vegan butter or olive oil in a small frying pan/skillet over high heat. Slice the pavs in half, and place in the hot pan so they soak up the butter or oil and start to fry slightly. (Alternatively, you can serve the rolls hot from the oven, drizzled with a little olive oil inside.) Pour a little of the vegetable mash into a small bowl, sprinkling a few onions and coriander/cilantro leaves on top. Add a squeeze of lemon or lime, and serve with the hot or toasted pav on the side.

BEETROOT AND WATERCRESS *samosas*

TO MAKE THE PASTRY
240 g/1¾ cups plain/
  all-purpose flour
1 teaspoon ajwain
  (carom) seeds
4 tablespoons vegetable
  oil
1 teaspoon sea salt
6 tablespoons water

TO MAKE THE FILLING
1 teaspoon cumin seeds
1 clove
4 black peppercorns
2 green cardamoms
½ teaspoon fennel seeds
1 teaspoon coriander
  seeds
1 tablespoon coconut or
  vegetable oil
5–7.5-cm/2–3-inch
  thumb of ginger, finely
  chopped

1–2 green chillies/
  chiles, to taste, finely
  chopped
1 teaspoon mild chilli/chili
  powder
1 teaspoon amchoor
  (green mango powder)
pinch of asafoetida (hing)
2–3 large beetroots/
  beets, boiled and
  peeled, cut into
  1-cm/⅜-inch cubes
bunch of watercress,
  roughly chopped
½ teaspoon salt, to taste
1 litre/4¼ cups vegetable
  oil, for deep-frying

MAKES 6–8

It's safe to say that we consumed a huge number of samosas during our travels in India and Nepal. Whether you are walking along the street or sitting on a train or bus, there's always a samosa to be had.

We ate these crispy filled pockets of spiced potato and pea from numerous roadside vendors, sitting on the banks of the Ganges and whilst waiting for many a train (stations in India are always superb places to enjoy great street food). Sometimes we ate them straight from the paper, or 'chaat' style in a little bamboo bowl with some sprouted chickpeas, tangy chutneys and sev (or 'Indian sprinkles' as we like to call them).

If you don't have a spice grinder to make the whole spice mix or are short on time, then you can just substitute some garam masala powder. You can buy whole cooked beetroot/beets to save time, too, but make sure it hasn't been pickled. If you buy whole beetroot/beets with the leaves, then you can also chop the leaves and add them to the filling along with the watercress.

I like to eat these samosas with a simple spicy pineapple and nigella seed chutney. It is the perfect combination of the plentiful (beetroot/beets) and the exotic (pineapple). It sounds a little different, but I promise you the flavours will make your mouth sing.

Above: Frying samosas, India.

Prepare the pastry by mixing together the flour, ajwain seeds, oil and salt. Rub together to create a crumb consistency. Add the water gradually, kneading together until you get a soft dough. Cover with a damp kitchen towel and leave to rest for 30 minutes.

Set aside ½ teaspoon of whole cumin seeds to use in the filling, then toast the rest of the whole spices for the samosa in a pan and then grind them to a fine powder (I use a coffee grinder, or you can use a pestle and mortar).

Heat the oil in a large frying pan/skillet or wok and add the ginger and green chilli/chile. Cook gently for about 2–3 minutes, then add the remaining ½ teaspoon whole cumin seeds, and cook for another 1–2 minutes until they start to crackle.

Add the freshly ground spice mix (or use 2 teaspoons garam masala) and then the chilli/chili

powder, amchoor, asafoetida and beetroot/beet cubes. Mix well and cook gently for 3–4 minutes. Remove from the heat and add the watercress and the salt to taste. Mix well and set aside to cool.

Knead the dough and divide into 6–8 equal balls. Lightly dust the work surface with flour and roll out the balls into large discs.

Cut each circle of pastry in half down the middle and take one half of the pastry into your hand. Brush some water down the straight edge and bring together those edges, like a cone, and seal them well.

Fill the cone of pastry with about a tablespoonful of filling, then dampen the edge and seal closed by pinching the top edges together. Repeat with the remaining dough to make 12–16 samosas (depending on how big you want to make them).

To fry the samosas, heat the vegetable oil for deep-frying in a deep pan. Drop a cube of bread into the oil to check that the oil is hot enough; it should sizzle immediately and rise to the surface.

Gently fry your samosas, in batches, for about 8 minutes, turning halfway through. Drain the samosas on paper towels, then keep them warm in a low oven while you cook the remaining batches. Alternatively, allow them to cool and then reheat later. They will keep in the fridge for several days.

For a healthier option, they can be baked for 30–40 minutes (180°C (350°F) Gas 4). Just brush them lightly with some oil prior to baking.

Serve warm with some chutney (see right) or cooling raita, and a cup of Indian masala (chai) tea.

Quick pineapple chutney

This is another very easy chutney to prepare and can be served alongside lots of different snacks and curries. This will keep for a few days in the fridge.

90 g/scant ½ cup granulated sugar
150 ml/⅔ cup rice vinegar
2 teaspoons nigella seeds
1 fresh red chilli/chile, finely chopped (or 1 teaspoon dried chilli flakes/hot red pepper flakes)
1 medium pineapple, peeled, cored and diced into 1.5-cm/½-inch pieces

MAKES 500 ML/2 CUPS

Add the sugar and rice vinegar to a medium pan, and place over low-medium heat. Bring to a simmer, dissolving all the sugar, then add the seeds and chilli/chile. Stir well and cook for a few minutes. Remove from the heat, add the pineapple and mix well. Set aside to cool, then spoon into sterilized jars and keep in the fridge.

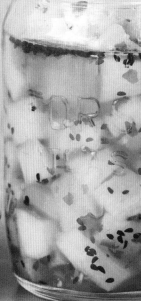

BOMBAY *vegetable sandwich*

There's so much amazing street food in India, it has a tendency to make sandwiches look rather boring. But the melting pot of Mumbai, with its Persian cafés and Portuguese rolls served with spicy mashed vegetables, was also the place we had our first proper Indian sandwich. Delicious and beautiful, the Mumbai vegetable sandwich is an icon of street food, and a lunchtime staple for many Mumbai office workers. Such an unassuming name I think – like it's trying to make us think it's not a salad sandwich when it is. It is totally packed with flavour and naturally vegan. There's a definite appeal for us Northerners too, with its carb on carb construction. As someone once joked, there's never enough carbs in a meal for a Northerner.

This vegan version packs all the flavours of green chutney and chaat spices with delicious vegetables, and should be served warm, or even better with a steaming cup of chai tea (see page 156). Traditionally it's filled with potato or sometimes beetroot/beet, and nearly always made with white bread and a slice of plastic-looking American-style cheese. I like potato and beetroot/beet together, on brown bread. The bits you shouldn't mess with are the coriander chutney and chaat masala spice. Both are essential. Indian sellers like to slather on the butter, perhaps to demonstrate some decadence, but more likely to stop the chutney making the bread go soggy. Just head to Nariman Point at lunchtime and you'll see the busy sandwich-walas toasting (or burning) them fresh to order and feeding hundreds of office workers. I prefer mine a little less blackened than the Mumbai versions, and with extra fresh tomato inside rather than ketchup slathered on top. Either way, it's all a delicious combination. And it makes a nice change from hummus!

1 potato, boiled in its skin for 20 minutes
1 beetroot/beet, boiled in its skin for 40 minutes
6 slices brown or white bread
1 tablespoon vegan butter or margarine (optional)
2 tomatoes, sliced
½ white onion, finely sliced
8 slices red (bell) pepper (optional)
8 slices cucumber (optional)
2 slices vegan cheese, such as Violife slices (optional)
2 pinches of chaat masala
½ tablespoon vegetable oil

TO MAKE THE 'GREEN' CHUTNEY
1 bunch of fresh coriander/cilantro
½ bunch of fresh mint
¼ small white onion
1–2 fresh green chillies/chiles
1 teaspoon brown sugar
2 tablespoons freshly squeezed lemon juice
pinch of salt

SERVES 2

Firstly, prepare the 'green' chutney, by blending together all of the ingredients with a stick blender or in a food processor. Cover and set aside.

Using gloved hands, rub the potato and beetroot/beet with your fingers to gently remove the skins. Cut into 5 mm/¼ inch thick slices.

Butter the bread on both sides, if you like. Starting with the bottom layer, slather green chutney onto the bread, then add the tomato slices and onion. Add sliced (bell) peppers and cucumber, if using, or a slice or two of vegan cheese, if you fancy.

Sprinkle lightly with chaat masala powder, then add another slice of bread. Lay the slices of potato and beetroot/beet on top and sprinkle with more chaat powder. Spread more green chutney on the last slice of bread and place on top of your double-decker sandwich. Repeat for the second sandwich.

Heat a frying pan/skillet over medium-high heat, then add the oil. Lay the sandwich carefully in the hot pan and toast on both sides, turning carefully so as not to spill the contents. Toast in the pan until golden brown. Repeat with second sandwich, then slice in half and serve warm.

SPINACH AND NASTURTIUM *kachori chaat*

When we first arrived in Kathmandu, it was a full-frontal assault on all the senses. At first it felt like going back in time in Northern India (at least how I imagined it). Fortunately, we were greeted by new friends who, despite only knowing me professionally (and online at that), were waiting in the arrivals hall to drive us into town. Biz and Parin helped us rent an apartment in Lazimpat, a residential suburb of Kathmandu, so we could immerse ourselves in local life and join in the fun of electricity bingo (usually meaning each area received only a handful of hours of electricity each day, although I'm sure our fancier apartment block got more than its fair share).

We also had a roof garden, where we appeared to be the only residents wanting to spend time up there, along with the building's resident dog, a Golden Labrador called Honey. The roof of any tall building in Kathmandu is one of the best ways to see the city and surrounding mountains on a clear day, but more often smog or clouds get in the way of this. On days like these, it's easy to forget that this bustling city is surrounded by impressive Himalayan peaks.

I grew very fond of our neighbourhood over the weeks. I would stop off for momos in a sidestreet café, pick up fresh samosas and kachori from the little local shops to take home, stock up on western treats in Blue Moon Grocery Store (along with local embassy staff) and admire the tiny allotments slotted in-between buildings, filled with cauliflower, beans and spinach. Nepal is primarily still a subsistence country, and even in the cities this remains important for many. But this comes into its own high in the mountains, where natural bounties of nettles or nasturtiums are made into delicious curries. Our Sherpa Pasang's nettle curry, gathered from around Rimchi guesthouse on a former trek route in the Langtang valley (since devastated by the 2015 earthquake), was truly an outstanding food moment in Nepal.

Kachori hail from Northern India, and are usually filled with a mixture of spiced black gram lentils or sometimes peas. I grow both spinach and nasturtiums in my garden, so this seems a fitting tribute to my Nepali friends and my Kathmandu kachori. You can eat them straight up (Kachori make a great portable snack), but I like to serve them chaat-style at home, with toppings, as it reminds me of Indian and Nepali festivities and celebrations. If there are sprinkles, it must be a party.

2 green chillies/chiles, finely chopped
2 plump garlic cloves
6.5-cm/2½-inch thumb of ginger, finely chopped (or 1 teaspoon ginger paste)
400 g/14 oz. fresh spinach, lightly wilted, or frozen spinach, defrosted and water squeezed out
200 g/7 oz. fresh nasturtium leaves or chard (or use extra spinach)
3 tablespoons coconut oil
1 teaspoon mustard seeds
½ teaspoon ground cinnamon
1 generous teaspoon garam masala
½ teaspoon ground turmeric
½ teaspoon chilli/chili powder
1–2 teaspoons salt, to taste
pinch of asafoetida (hing, optional)
1 tablespoon chickpea/garbanzo bean flour (gram flour)

TO MAKE THE PASTRY

300 g/2¼ cups plain/all-purpose
 flour
½ teaspoon salt
2 tablespoons olive oil
175 ml/¾ cup warm water

TO MAKE THE TOPPINGS

handful of sprouted beans or
 lentils (optional)
chutney of choice, such as
 coriander 'green' chutney
 (see page 114)
handful of thin sev (little fried
 gram sticks)
handful of fresh pomegranate
 seeds
¼ red onion, finely sliced
pinch of chaat powder (optional)
drizzle of plain vegan yogurt
drizzle of pomegranate molasses
 (optional)

MAKES 8–10

*Below: Local farmer
selling vegetables.*

Preheat the oven to 160°C (325°F) Gas 3.

Using a hand blender or a food processor, blitz the chillies/chiles, garlic and ginger to a paste. Set aside. In the same processor, blitz the spinach and nasturtium leaves.

Heat the coconut oil in a small frying pan/skillet and fry the mustard seeds until they start to splutter, then add the chilli/chile, ginger and garlic paste and fry for a few minutes. Add the spinach mixture along with the cinnamon, garam masala, turmeric, chilli/chili powder, salt and asafoetida, and simmer on a low-medium heat for 15–20 minutes until most of the liquid has evaporated. Remove from the heat and add the chickpea/garbanzo bean flour (gram flour). Mix well and set aside.

To make the pastry, add the flour, salt and oil to a bowl and rub together with your fingers. Add the warm water so the dough comes together, and remains quite firm. Knead well for a few minutes.

Pour a little oil into your hands and rub it all over the dough ball. Take a large pinch of the dough and roll it into a golf ball-sized ball. On a floured surface, roll out the ball into a 10-cm/4-inch circle. Place a spoonful of the filling in the middle, then bring up the edges over the filling to the centre and pinch to seal the top, removing any excess pastry if necessary. Using the palm of your hand, gently flatten the filled dough slightly to make a thick circular disc. Repeat with the remaining dough and filling. (You can also roll them into ball shapes, but this is less effective for chaat-style serving.)

The kachori can be fried, but I prefer to bake them for a slightly lighter snack. Using lightly oiled hands, coat the outside of the kachori a little with oil, or use an oil spray. Place on a baking sheet and bake in the oven for 20–30 minutes until the pastry is golden brown and crisped.

To serve, lay the kachori onto a serving platter in a single layer, and using a knife, make a circular hole in the top of each one, about 2.5 cm/1 inch wide. Be sure to cut only the top layer of pastry. Next add some sprouted beans, if using, into the hole, along with a little blob or two of chutney. Then sprinkle the top of the pastries with strands of sev, pomegranate seeds, chopped red onion and chaat powder, if using. Drizzle with vegan yogurt and pomegranate molasses, if you like.

BEETROOT *pakoda kadhi*

This is one of my all-time favourite comfort dishes. Based on the traditional Punjabi (and Gujarati) dish known as 'kadhi' (pronounced kaddy), you don't see this very often on Indian-British menus, aside from the occasional special in a traditional dhaba café.

We first came across this dish in the dhabas of Amritsar, a holy Sikh city in the heart of the Punjab region and a stone's throw from the Pakistan border. I tried to make this dish in a windy tent in Peckham Rye on MasterChef. The dish was a disaster for many reasons, but my meltdown made good TV. Despite this, I refused to let it go, and developed a recipe to serve at my supperclub and eventually on the Hungry Gecko menu. Two regulars loved it so much they asked me to include it on their wedding menu.

I sometimes make a healthier version by baking pakoda 'dumplings' in the oven instead of frying. You could substitute the beetroot/beets for other vegetables, if you prefer. I use a vegan coconut-based plain yogurt for this as it has a nice creamy texture but you can use whichever type you prefer – just make sure it's not sweet. The sour note is important in the kadhi sauce. You can use ready-cooked beetroot/beets to save time, but ensure it isn't pickled.

TO MAKE THE PAKODA DUMPLINGS
- 1–2 tablespoons vegetable oil
- 1 onion, thinly sliced
- 3 medium beetroots/beets, cooked and cut into 2-cm/¾-inch cubes
- 2–4 small green chillies/chiles, finely chopped
- 1 tablespoon red chilli/chili powder
- ½ teaspoon asafoetida (hing)
- 150 g/1⅔ cups chickpea/garbanzo bean flour (gram flour), sifted
- 2 teaspoons cumin seeds
- 2 tablespoons fennel seeds
- 300–500 ml/1¼–2 cups cold water
- 2 tablespoons dried pomegranate seeds (optional)
- 1 bunch of fresh coriander/cilantro, roughly chopped
- ½ teaspoon bicarbonate of soda/baking soda
- 1 teaspoon salt
- about 400 ml/scant 1¾ cups pomace or vegetable oil, for deep-frying

TO MAKE THE KADHI SAUCE
- 280 ml/scant 1¼ cups unsweetened coconut yogurt
- 1½ tablespoons chickpea/garbanzo bean flour (gram flour)
- 750 ml/3 cups water
- 1 tablespoon ground coriander, lightly toasted
- 1 teaspoon ground turmeric
- 1–2 teaspoons salt, to taste

FOR THE TEMPERING
- 1 teaspoon mustard seeds
- pinch of asafoetida (hing)
- 1–2 whole red chillies/chiles, to taste, broken into pieces
- 4 garlic cloves, finely sliced
- 1–2 green chillies/chiles, deseeded and sliced lengthways (optional)
- handful of fresh or dried curry leaves (optional)

TO SERVE
- steamed basmati rice
- warm chapattis

SERVES 4

Preheat the oven to 180°C (350°F) Gas 4.

Heat the oil in a small frying pan/skillet and sauté the onion gently for 7 minutes until well softened. Add the cooked beetroot/beets, chopped fresh chillies/chiles, chilli/chili powder and asafoetida, and cook for a further 2 minutes. Set aside.

Sift the chickpea/garbanzo bean flour (gram flour) into a large bowl. Roast the cumin and fennel seeds in a dry pan, taking care not to burn the spices, then add to the flour along with the onion and beetroot/beet mixture. Add 300 ml/1¼ cups of the cold water to make a thick paste, then add the pomegranate seeds, coriander/cilantro, bicarbonate of soda/baking soda and salt, and mix well. Add more water as necessary to create a thick batter with a porridge-/oatmeal-like consistency.

To fry the pakoda dumplings, fill a pan about 6–7 cm/2½ inches deep with the vegetable oil, and place over medium-high heat. Once the oil is sizzling hot (test with a small pinch of batter, it should sizzle not burn), gently drop spoonfuls of the mixture into the oil. Fry for 7–8 minutes until golden brown, then drain on paper towels. Fry the pakoda in batches, and keep them warm in the oven while finishing the sauce.

(Alternatively, if you want to bake the pakoda, use a dessert spoon to drop spoonfuls of the mixture gently onto a well-oiled baking tray, ensuring the pakoda are well spaced apart. Place in the oven at 180°C (350°F) Gas 4 and bake for 8–10 minutes, then remove and brush with a little oil. Return the dumplings to the oven for another 8–10 minutes, until cooked through.)

To make the sauce, mix 2–3 tablespoons of the yogurt with the chickpea/garbanzo bean flour (gram flour) in a large deep frying pan/skillet or wok to make a smooth paste. Then add the remaining yogurt, water, ground coriander and turmeric. Whisk well over medium heat while bringing to the boil. Simmer gently for 3–4 minutes until the flour mixture has cooked through and the sauce has thickened. Add a little more water, if necessary, to make a thick pouring consistency. Set aside.

Place the tempering ingredients into a small frying pan/skillet and fry over high heat for a few minutes until the seeds splutter. Tip the tempering into the sauce mixture. Stir well and season with salt to taste.

Gently lay the cooked dumplings in the sauce and bring to a gentle simmer. Stir gently and be careful not break the dumplings. Add a little more water to the sauce if necessary, to ensure a smooth gravy-like consistency.

Serve with steamed basmati rice and some warm chapatti for mopping up the sauce. Indian comfort food pure and simple!

NO SHIMI *shami kebab*

Shami kebabs appear to be everywhere. They always serve them in the Pakistani cafés along the curry mile in Manchester, and we often saw them across the Punjab region in India. Except we didn't eat any because they were always made with meat. This recipe is packed with flavours and uses textured vegetable protein (TVP) to give more texture and bite. These spicy cakes can be served in a 'pav' roll (see page 108) for an Indian-style vegan burger (vada pao), but I prefer to serve them in a soft naan with crunchy salad, minted yogurt and hot sauce. Perhaps the perfect substitute for the post-pub dirty kebab/kabob, except it's delicious and plant-powered.

TO MAKE THE SHAMI PATTIES

100 g/3½ oz. soya or TVP mince, dried
½ teaspoon yeast extract
1 slice brown bread
120 g/⅔ cup channa dal (split yellow peas), soaked overnight
1 large potato, peeled, boiled and mashed
½ tablespoon chickpea/garbanzo bean flour (gram flour)
3 tablespoons freshly chopped coriander/cilantro
1 carrot, peeled and grated
1 green chilli/chile, finely chopped
1 tablespoon dried methi leaves (fenugreek)
½ teaspoon dried chilli flakes/hot red pepper flakes
2 teaspoons garam masala, lightly toasted
1 teaspoon ground coriander, lightly toasted
2 tablespoons pomace or coconut oil

TO SERVE

4 fluffy naan breads, warm (see page 124)
7–8 large lettuce leaves, roughly torn
1 small red onion, thinly sliced
2 tomatoes, halved and thickly sliced
3–4 tablespoons vegan yogurt, such as coconut yogurt
3–4 tablespoons Burmese-style hot sauce (see page 136) or other hot sauce
handful of fresh coriander/cilantro or mint leaves, to garnish (optional)
handful of pomegranate seeds, to garnish (optional)

SERVES 4

Soak the dried TVP or soya in boiling water with the yeast extract for 15 minutes. In a food processor, blitz the bread into crumbs and place in a large bowl.

Drain the TVP or soya mince and squeeze out the excess liquid. Drain the dal, ensuring no excess water is left. Blitz the dal in the food processor and add to the breadcrumbs along with the TVP or soya mince, mashed potato, chickpea/garbanzo bean flour (gram flour), coriander/cilantro, grated carrot, chilli/chile, dried methi leaves, dried chilli flakes/hot red pepper flakes, garam masala and ground coriander. Using your hands, mix well to bring all the ingredients together. Divide into 8 balls and then shape into little patties, about 7 cm/3 inches wide and 2 cm/¾ inch thick.

Heat the oil in a large frying pan/skillet and fry the patties in batches, three or four at a time, turning once until golden brown on both sides. Keep the patties warm in a low oven while you prepare and cook the naan breads.

To construct your take-out style kebab/kabob, add lettuce leaves, onion and tomatoes onto the warm bread. Add two or three shami patties, then slather on some yogurt along with chilli/chili sauce. Scatter with some fresh coriander/cilantro or mint and pomegranate seeds when serving, if you like.

The secret to excellent naan is in the resting. If you make the dough the day before, and allow the second proving to take place overnight, it will be even more fluffy.

EASY FLUFFY *naan*

1 teaspoon active dry yeast
120 ml/½ cup warm water
1 tablespoon sugar
240 g/1¾ cups strong bread flour
3 tablespoons soy or oat milk
1 teaspoon salt
2 tablespoons olive oil

MAKES 4

Mix the yeast with half of the warm water and the sugar in a mixing bowl. Set aside until it starts to get frothy, then add the rest of the water with the remaining ingredients and knead well for 5–10 minutes to form a soft, stretchy dough.

Lightly oil your hands and cover the dough with oil. Place it in a bowl with a damp kitchen towel over the top and set aside for 30–60 minutes to rise, until it has doubled in size. The time will depend on how warm the room is.

Once it has doubled in size, punch down the dough and knead again, then roll into four 6–7-cm/2¾-inch balls. Place the lightly oiled balls onto a baking sheet, spaced well apart, and leave to rise again for at least 1 hour, or preferably overnight.

Use your hands to roll out the dough balls on a well-floured surface, stretching and flattening them gently but firmly until they are about 1–1.5cm/½ inch thick.

Lightly oil a large baking sheet, and stretch out the naan onto the sheet. Place under very hot grill/broiler, cooking for a few minutes each side. Allow the first side to start bubbling before brushing the top lightly with oil, then turning once to cook the other side until it's nicely bubbled with a few browned edges and bubbles. It should be soft, and not brown all over.

Above: Making naan breads over a tandoor.

PEA AND METHI *stuffed parathas*

A well-made stuffed paratha is a thing of beauty. The real deal bears no relation to the greasy takeaway versions often served in the UK. It's less work than you think to make your own, which will far more likely resemble a good Indian breakfast. Traditionally it is served with curd, but coconut yogurt or simple dal is a fine accompaniment. You can pretty much grate any vegetable to stuff into a paratha, but this combination is incredibly flavoursome. It's worth seeking out some fresh methi from an Indian or Pakistani grocer.

TO MAKE THE DOUGH
240 g/1¾ cups fine wholemeal (whole-wheat) flour
½ teaspoon ajwain (carom) seeds
½ teaspoon fine salt
1 teaspoon pomace or vegetable oil
about 60 ml/4 tablespoons warm water

TO MAKE THE FILLING
160 g/1¼ cups frozen peas
bunch of fresh methi leaves (fenugreek), roughly chopped
½ teaspoon cumin seeds
¼ tablespoon chickpea/garbanzo bean flour (gram flour)
1 tablespoon freshly chopped coriander/cilantro
1–3 fresh green chillies, to taste, finely chopped
pinch of asafoetida (hing, optional)
½ teaspoon garam masala
1 teaspoon fine salt

TO COOK AND SERVE
2–3 tablespoons coconut oil
coconut yogurt or dhaba-style dal (see page 104)

MAKES 2

To prepare the dough, mix together the flour, ajwain and salt in a large bowl, then add the oil and enough of the warm water to make a soft, pliable dough. You can add more flour if it is too sticky (paratha-making is not an exact science). Knead well for 5–10 minutes, then cover and set aside for 30 minutes.

Roll the dough into four (or five if your pan is smaller) chunky golf ball-sized balls, then rest again for 5–10 minutes.

Heat the peas and chopped methi in a small pan for a few minutes, ensuring they are softened slightly. Roughly mash the peas and methi leaves, then place in a sieve/strainer and squeeze out any excess water.

Lightly toast the cumin seeds in a wok or frying pan/skillet. Add the chickpea/garbanzo bean flour (gram flour) and toast until it is aromatic and changes colour slightly. Don't let it burn by browning too much.

Add the pea and methi mixture to the pan and mash a little more if needed. Remove from the heat and set aside to cool slightly. Add the remaining ingredients and mix well.

On a well-floured surface, roll out the dough balls to about 16–18 cm/6–7 inches in diameter. Lay half of the vegetable mixture on one of the discs, ensuring a 2-cm/¾-inch gap around the edge. Dampen the space left around the edge with a little water and place a second disc on top. Fold the edge of the bottom paratha over onto the top paratha and push down to seal the edges. Repeat with the other two discs of dough and the remaining filling to make two big parathas.

Place a large frying pan/skillet or tawa over medium heat and cook the parathas, one at a time. Allow the first side to cook until it has a few well-browned patches (it doesn't have to be browned all over). Turn it over and spoon a little coconut oil over the top, spreading it over the cooked side with the back of the spoon. Flip again and brush on some more oil. Keep the paratha warm in a low oven while cooking the second one.

Serve with a big bowl of coconut yogurt for an Indian-style breakfast or with a big bowl of dhaba-style dal.

BOMBAY FRANKIE
Masala vegetable roti wrap

This hugely popular street food snack originates from 1930s Bombay, as a spiced potato or vegetable roti wrap. Like Kolkata's meaty kati roll, an egg is sometimes added to the bread as it is cooking. Both are roti wraps in some form though. These days, both have many different fillings, and I created a recipe for the Hungry Gecko menu fairly early on. It was always hugely popular at festivals as it's the perfect thing to eat single-handedly. I like to think of them as India's answer to the burrito.

You can adapt the main vegetable in the masala to suit your preference or the seasons. Potato or cauliflower both work well. I sometimes use aubergine/eggplant pickle or sweet mango chutney from a jar, but you could use whatever you prefer.

TO MAKE THE SLAW
¼ small white cabbage, finely sliced
¼ small red cabbage, finely sliced
freshly squeezed juice of 2 limes or lemons
about 1 tablespoon brown sugar or agave syrup
1 fresh red chilli/chile, finely chopped (optional)
½–1 teaspoon fine salt, to taste

TO MAKE THE FILLING
2 small aubergines/ eggplants, cut into 3–4-cm/1½-inch pieces (or use 2 large waxy potatoes, diced and parboiled until just cooked)
1 brown onion, cut into 3–4-cm/1½-inch pieces
1 green (bell) pepper, cut into 3–4-cm/1½-inch pieces
2 tablespoons garam masala
½ teaspoon chilli/chili powder
1 teaspoon rock salt
3 tablespoons coconut oil

TO ASSEMBLE AND SERVE
4 large desi paratha
2–3 tablespoons mango or pear chutney, or whichever chutney you prefer
plain vegan yogurt
handful of fresh mint and coriander/cilantro
1–2 fresh green chillies/ chiles, finely sliced (optional)

SERVES 4

Prepare the slaw by mixing together all the ingredients into a large bowl, then cover and set aside for at least 30 minutes, but preferably 1–2 hours, so that the cabbages soften in the juice and sugars. Check the seasoning and add more salt, chilli/ chile or sugar as you prefer.

In a medium pan, add all the ingredients for the filling and place over medium-high heat. Stir well, bring to a simmer and then lower the heat. Cook for about 10–15 minutes until the vegetables are soft.

Warm the paratha on both sides in a large frying pan/skillet or tawa. Spread a generous layer of chutney onto the bread, then layer on some slaw and 2–3 spoonfuls of the masala vegetables on top. Leave enough space on the bread so you can wrap the frankie. Drizzle with some yogurt and sprinkle with herbs and fresh chillies/chiles, if you like.

Serving this on the Gecko, we placed a piece of foil or baking parchment on the chopping board and constructed the frankie on top, keeping all the filling in a long rectangle down the centre of the bread. To fold, lift and fold in the bottom 3–5 cm/1–2 inches of the bread, then fold in each side, one at a time, firmly but gently, ensuring the filling is snugly wrapped, and leaving the top open. Wrap the foil or parchment around the sides of the bread to hold it in place, covering the bottom so the juices don't leak, but leaving the top open. Serve with a napkin!

THAI-STYLE REDCAKES
Spicy 'crab cakes' with heart of palm

I can thank Crossroads Kitchen in LA for introducing me to heart of palm. It's a popular vegetable in South America, mostly tinned, and widely available in the UK. It's important to source this ingredient from sustainable farms, as wild harvesting is damaging to the environment. It is mostly farmed in Costa Rica and Hawaii. The menu at Crossroads included 'calamari' made with heart of palm rings and 'crab cakes' made with seaweed. I've been using seaweed for a while now for that taste of the sea, but this vegetable was a revelation. When I got home, I decided to make something a bit punchier in flavour. This red curry paste can be used to make a Thai red curry or even a spicy vegetable soup. Simply add coconut milk, stock and whatever vegetables you prefer.

2 tablespoons coconut oil

2 banana shallots, finely chopped

340-g/12-oz. can heart of palms, drained and patted dry

2 floury potatoes, such as Maris Piper or Yukon Gold, boiled in their skins until soft

½ sheet nori, finely chopped

1–2 teaspoons potato flour or cornflour/cornstarch, plus extra for dusting

handful of freshly chopped coriander/cilantro

½ teaspoon fine salt

3 tablespoons panko breadcrumbs, plus 90 g/2 cups, for coating

2 tablespoons flax 'egg' (see page 15) or egg replacer

coconut or vegetable oil, for frying

potato flour, plain flour or cornflour/cornstarch, for dusting

TO MAKE THE RED CURRY PASTE

1 tablespoon coriander seeds

1 teaspoon cumin seeds

1 teaspoon black peppercorns

4 garlic cloves, peeled

3 coriander roots or the stems from ½ bunch of fresh coriander/cilantro

10–12 dried red chillies/chiles

2 lemongrass stalks, chopped

4–5 kaffir lime leaves

7.5-cm/3-inch piece galangal or ginger, peeled and chopped

2 tablespoons vegan fish sauce or light soy sauce

1 tablespoon vegetable oil, plus extra if needed

TO SERVE

lettuce leaves

sweet or hot chilli/chili dipping sauce

lime wedges

MAKES 6–8

To make the red curry paste, toast the coriander and cumin seeds in a small pan until aromatic. Then grind the seeds along with the peppercorns to make a powder. Place the remaining red curry paste ingredients in a blender along with the toasted spices, and blend to a smooth paste, adding a little extra oil if necessary. Store in a sterilized glass jar.

Heat ½ tablespoon of the coconut oil in a small pan, add the shallots and fry over medium-high heat until softened. Add 1 tablespoon red curry paste, cook for a few minutes, then remove from the heat.

Roughly chop the washed and dried hearts of palm. Peel the skin from the cooked potatoes and empty into a large bowl. Mash well with a fork. Add the shallot mixture, chopped nori, potato flour, coriander/cilantro, salt and the 3 tablespoons breadcrumbs. Using gloved hands, mix well to combine everything. Fold in the hearts of palm.

Form the dough into 6–8 little patties and dust with potato flour. Dip the patties in the flax 'egg' and then dip in the remaining breadcrumbs to give an even crust. Place a large frying pan/skillet over medium-high heat, with the remaining 1½ tablespoons coconut oil. Shallow fry the patties, in batches, for 4–5 minutes on each side, until they are golden brown on both sides. Drain on paper towels.

Serve the cakes with lettuce leaves, sweet chilli/chili dipping sauce and a wedge of lime on the side.

BUS STATION RICE
Thai-style vegetable rice

Bus stations are one of the great places to meet interesting people on the road. Case in point. On a more recent trip to Thailand in early 2015, we were waiting for our bus to take us to the coastal town of Ranong near the Myanmar border. Engulfed amongst some uncrossable highways, we were the captive audience of the Thai bus station, with its funny little stalls, cafés and strange smells. Bus station rice is always a good option in these situations.

In truth, Lee and I love this part of travelling. Especially when we connect with people, share a few hours of intense conversation, thoughts and food and then go on our way. Rarely do we see or hear from each other again. But sometimes we do. We spent many travel hours with Eva-Lotta and her partner Nathaniel on the road to Ranong and beyond. Her travel diaries focus on illustration and utilising our brain's natural mind-mapping structures to record experiences and observations.

As a former sociologist, I am fascinated by her work and her diary brilliantly depicts our journey that day.

Back to the rice. The key ingredient is to use a good roasted Thai chilli/chili sambal or nam prik pao, which is the fiery, dark and sticky Thai chilli/chili jam, rather than the orange-coloured sweet variety. You could substitute the Burmese-style hot sauce (see page 136), as this is super quick to prepare from scratch. I also recommend using a pestle and mortar for this dish, so you get smashed garlic rather than purée. Thai cooks will use whatever vegetables are in season, so you can mix it up with your ingredients.

3 tablespoons coconut oil
4 garlic cloves, crushed and chopped
1 banana shallot, finely chopped
handful of fine green beans, cut into 2.5-cm/1-inch pieces
1 carrot, peeled and diced
handful of finely sliced white cabbage
2 tablespoons light soy sauce or vegan fish sauce
2 tablespoons Thai chilli/chili jam, sambal or sriracha

280 g/2½ cups cooked basmati or jasmine rice, chilled
handful of frozen peas and soy beans
70 g/½ cup red skinned peanuts, lightly toasted
handful of freshly chopped coriander/cilantro, to garnish
lime wedges, to serve

SERVES 2–3

Heat 2 tablespoons of the coconut oil in a large wok over high heat. Add the garlic, fry for 2 minutes and then add the chopped shallot, green beans and carrot. Fry for a further 2–3 minutes, then add the cabbage, soy sauce and Thai chilli jam.

Once the mixture is hot and sizzling, move it to one side of pan and then add the rice, peas and soy beans. Add the remaining 1 tablespoon of coconut oil to the rice mixture, and cook for a further 4–5 minutes over high heat, carefully moving the rice until it starts to crisp a little, then mix well.

Add more chilli/chili jam, if needed, to ensure the rice and vegetables are all well coated and adjust to taste for heat and seasoning, adding salt if needed.

Serve immediately, sprinkled with toasted peanuts and some roughly chopped fresh coriander/cilantro, and with a wedge of lime on the side.

KHMER CROQUETTES *with spring vegetables*

This recipe gives a little nod to Cambodia's French protectorate history together with a wallop of authentic Khmer spicing from the yellow curry paste. The pickled vegetables add a fragrant South East Asian twist and means I get to use my favourite Kampot peppercorns. Serve these pickles alongside your favourite fried snacks or rice dish.

½ tablespoon vegetable or coconut oil

2 tablespoons yellow curry paste (see page 140)

1 leek, washed and finely sliced

3–4 spring onions/scallions, trimmed and sliced

60 g/½ cup frozen peas

2–3 large floury potatoes, such as Maris Piper or Yukon Gold, boiled and mashed

45 g/1 cup panko breadcrumbs

2–3 tablespoons cornflour/cornstarch

2–3 tablespoons soy cream or flax 'egg' (see page 15)

200 ml/scant 1 cup vegetable oil, for frying

Cambodian-style pickled vegetables (see right)

chilli/chili sambal, to serve

SERVES 3–4

Cambodian-style pickled vegetables

200 g/7 oz. carrots, peeled

200 g/7 oz. mooli/daikon, peeled

200 g/7 oz. cucumber, halved and deseeded

125 ml/½ cup water

125 ml/½ cup rice vinegar

3 teaspoons rock or sea salt, plus extra to cover the vegetables

55 g/4½ tablespoons sugar

2 teaspoons black peppercorns, preferably Kampot

lemongrass stalks, ends trimmed, outer layer removed and finely sliced

3–4-cm/1¼–1½-inch thumb of ginger, peeled and chopped

MAKES 500 ML/2 CUPS

Heat the oil in a frying pan/skillet and gently fry the yellow curry paste for 5–6 minutes. Add the leek and cook gently for 3–4 minutes until starting to soften. Add the spring onions/scallions and cook for a further 1 minute. Mix in the peas. Remove from the heat.

Combine the mashed potato in a bowl with the curry mixture using gloved hands. Place the panko breadcrumbs on one plate and the cornflour/cornstarch on another. Place the soy cream in a bowl.

Using gloved hands, shape the potato into golf ball-sized balls. Dip the potato into the cornflour/cornstarch and then into the soy cream. Gently roll the croquette in the breadcrumbs until well coated.

Heat the vegetable oil in a frying pan/skillet to 190°C (375°F). Test the temperature by dropping a few breadcrumbs into the oil; if it sizzles, it is ready. Carefully fry the croquettes in the hot oil in batches, turning occasionally until golden brown on all sides. Drain on paper towels. Keep them warm in a low oven while you cook the remaining batches. Serve with some pickled vegetables and chilli/chili sambal.

Using a potato peeler, slice the vegetables into thin ribbons and place in a large bowl. Cover with salt and mix well so all the vegetables are well coated. Leave to sit for 30–40 minutes.

Rinse the vegetables in a colander, then pat dry with paper towels. Place the vegetables in a large sterilized jar.

In a pan, mix together the water, vinegar, sugar, the 3 teaspoons salt, peppercorns, sliced lemongrass and ginger. Bring to a simmer, stir well and then remove from the heat. Cool for 30 minutes, then pour over the vegetables.

Make sure all the vegetables are well covered with the pickling liquid. Seal the lid and place in the fridge for a few hours before eating. The pickles will keep for a few weeks in the fridge.

LOTUS ROOT *with Burmese-style hot sauce*

One of my favourite food journeys in Thailand started in the fantastically friendly and colourful border town of Mae Sot. The road from here broadly follows the Myanmar/Burmese border north onto Mae Sariang and then Mae Hong Son. We finally rested our weary legs in the town of Pai, a hillside hippy enclave about 120 km/75 miles northwest of Chang Mai. The area is incredibly ethnically diverse, with hill tribes of Thailand and Burma, such as Hmong, Lisu, Karen and Shan, as well as Burmese Muslims and Chinese, which has a huge influence on the food.

We all loved Mae Sot, with its bustling markets, Burmese curries and fritters, and incredible salads. We ate a lot of delicious fried snacks along the way such as shan tofu and Burmese-style pakoras; delicious and portable food for a 9-hour 'song-thaew' journey (a shared taxi pick-up truck with a plastic roof over two facing benches). A kicking chilli/chili and garlic sauce is nearly always served on the side. If you can't get lotus root, use crunchy vegetables such as carrots, cauliflower or turnips.

1 tablespoon self-raising/self-rising flour
1 tablespoon rice flour
½ tablespoon chickpea/garbanzo bean flour (gram flour)
¼ teaspoon baking powder
1 tablespoon garam masala powder
½ teaspoon rock salt
180 ml/¾ cup sparkling/soda water
about 500 ml/2 cups vegetable oil, for deep-frying
1 lotus root bulb, peeled and cut into 4–5 mm/⅜ inch thick slices

TO MAKE THE HOT SAUCE
40 g/1½ oz. dried large red chillies/chiles, roughly torn
6 garlic cloves
300 ml/1¼ cups cold water
50 ml/3½ tablespoons vegan fish sauce, light soy or tamari
50 g/¼ cup brown sugar
150 ml/⅔ cup rice vinegar

SERVES 3–4

To make the quick dipping sauce, add the chillies/chiles, garlic and water to a small pan, bring to the boil and simmer gently for 5–10 minutes. Remove from the heat, then add the vegan fish, sugar and rice vinegar. Blend the mixture using a stick blender or food processor. Return to the heat and simmer for 3–4 minutes until starting to thicken. Leave to cool.

Whisk together the flours, baking powder, garam masala, salt and sparkling/soda water to make a smooth batter. Leave to stand for 10 minutes.

Add the vegetable oil to a medium pan and heat over medium-high heat. Check the oil is hot enough by dropping a little batter into the hot oil and making sure it sizzles.

Working in small batches of 4 or 5 pieces, dip the lotus root slices into the batter and gently place them in the hot oil. Fry for 7–8 minutes until golden brown and crispy on both sides. Drain on paper towels.

Serve immediately, as a snack or appetizer, accompanied by the Burmese-style hot sauce.

SINGAPOREAN LAKSA
Katong-style

Curry laksa is a spicy coconut broth version with
yellow or rice noodles and lots of toppings. Top this
laksa with a Thai-style redcake (see page 131) and
some quirky 'calamari'-style hearts of palm.

TO MAKE THE SPICE PASTE

1 small red onion
8 garlic cloves
2 5-cm/2-inch thumbs of fresh
   turmeric
6.5-cm/2½-inch thumb of fresh
   galangal (or use extra ginger)
6.5 cm/2½-inch thumb of ginger
5–10 dried large red chillies/chiles,
   to taste, soaked in hot water
   for 20 minutes and drained
6 lemongrass stalks, ends trimmed
   and outer layer removed
10 macadamia nuts
4 tablespoons vegetable oil

TO MAKE THE BROTH

1 litre/4¼ cups vegetable stock
1 tablespoon molasses
2 tablespoons vegan fish sauce
1 tablespoon ground coriander
1–2 teaspoons salt, to taste
1 bunch of laksa leaves, including
   stems (or coriander/cilantro)
400-ml/14-oz. can coconut milk
2–3 tablespoons chilli/chili sambal
200 g/7 oz. tofu puffs, halved
4 Thai-style redcakes (see page 131)
1 cucumber
100 g/3½ oz. thin yellow vegan
   'egg' noodles, soaked in boiling
   water for 15–20 minutes
250 g/scant 4½ cups bean sprouts
4 limes, halved
coriander/cilantro and mint leaves,
   to garnish

TO MAKE THE CALAMARI RINGS (OPTIONAL)

200 g/7 oz. heart of palm 'rings',
1 tablespoon rice flour
1 tablespoon potato flour
1 tablespoon plain/all-purpose flour
1 heaped teaspoon Korean red
   pepper powder
½ teaspoon salt
250 ml/1 cup sparkling/soda water
300–400 ml/1¼–scant 1¾ cups
   vegetable oil, for frying

SERVES 3–4

To make the spice paste (or rempah), blitz together the onions, garlic, fresh turmeric, galangal, ginger, drained chillies, lemongrass and nuts with 2 tablespoons of the oil to make a fairly smooth paste.

Place a heavy-bottomed pan over medium-high heat, add the remaining 2 tablespoons of oil and then fry the paste, stirring well to prevent it burning, for 10–15 minutes until well cooked and fragrant.

Add the stock, molasses, vegan fish sauce, ground coriander and salt, and bring to a simmer for a few minutes. Roughly tear the laksa leaves and add to the broth along with stems. Bring to a simmer and then add the coconut milk, sambal and tofu puffs. Bring back to the boil and simmer for 2–3 minutes before removing from the heat. Remove the woody stems from the broth.

Prepare and cook the Thai-style redcakes, and cut into bitesize pieces. Set aside in a warm oven until ready to use.

To make the 'calamari'-style rings, rinse and drain the heart of palm stems on paper towels. Slice into 2.5-cm/1-inch rounds. Carefully push out the centre of the ring with a small fingertip (this flaky part is perfect for making the Thai-style redcakes). Repeat with the other rounds.

Mix the rice, potato and plain/all-purpose flours together in a small bowl, add the salt and Korean pepper powder. Add 150 ml/⅔ cup of the sparkling/soda water and mix well to form a runny batter that should coat the back of a spoon. Add more sparkling/soda water, if needed.

Heat the oil for frying in a small pan. Check the oil temperature with small drop of batter; it should sizzle but not burn. Dip the rings into the batter and carefully drop into the hot oil, frying for 2–3 minutes until the batter is golden and crispy. Set aside on paper towels.

Cut the cucumber lengthways, and, using a small spoon, scoop out the seeds down the centre. Using a sharp knife, cut the cucumber into large matchsticks, and set aside.

Blanch the noodles in boiling water to reheat and lay a handful into each serving bowl. Blanch the bean sprouts and scatter half on top of the noodles. Then ladle on the broth so the noodles and sprouts are well covered. Then top with the remaining bean sprouts, cucumber strips, 'calamari'-style rings and the Thai-style redcakes. Squeeze fresh lime over the top and add to the bowl along with some coriander/cilantro and mint leaves.

NUM BANH CHOK
Cambodian yellow curry with rice noodles

We ate like royalty in Phnom Penh, and it's a city I would happily spend months exploring and eating my way around. My favourite dishes include Khmer yellow curry, rich with turmeric and lemongrass, and flavourful summer rolls stuffed with crunchy vegetables and fresh basil, mint and coriander/cilantro. The French influences are still apparent, and European restaurants are widespread. This soupy curry is traditionally served with slippery rice noodles and some crispy banana flower, but I also like it with sticky rice for mopping up the sauce. The yellow paste will keep for several weeks in the fridge.

TO MAKE THE SPICE PASTE
2 6-cm/2¼-inch thumbs of fresh turmeric (or 1½ teaspoons powdered)
½ teaspoon paprika
4 garlic cloves
5-cm/2-inch thumb of ginger
5-cm/2-inch thumb of galangal
4–6 dried red chillies/chiles, soaked in boiling water for 15 minutes
1 small red onion
2 lemongrass stalks, ends trimmed and outer layer removed
10 kaffir lime leaves

TO MAKE THE CRISPY BANANA FLOWER
1–2 tablespoons cornflour/cornstarch
½ teaspoon salt
½ banana flower, finely sliced into rings (or artichoke heart)
2 tablespoons coconut oil

TO MAKE THE CURRY
2 tablespoons coconut or vegetable oil
900 ml/scant 4 cups vegetable stock or water, plus extra if needed
2–3 tablespoons vegan fish sauce or light soy sauce
1 tablespoon brown sugar or agave syrup
200 g/7 oz. lotus root, peeled and cut into thick slices (or use cauliflower florets)
½ butternut squash, peeled and cubed
150 g/5½ oz. green beans, trimmed
400-ml/14-oz. can coconut milk
1–2 teaspoons rock salt, to taste
100 g/3½ oz. Chinese leaf, roughly torn (or chard, beet leaves or other greens)

TO SERVE
1 packet of thin rice thread noodles, soaked in hand-hot water for 30 minutes
drizzle of chilli/chili oil (optional)
50 g/½ cup roasted peanuts, roughly chopped (optional)

SERVES 3–4

Place all the spice paste ingredients in a blender or food processor and blitz until it forms a nice smooth paste.

To make the crispy banana flower, place the cornflour/cornstarch and salt in a bowl and toss the banana flower pieces in the flour until well coated. Heat the coconut oil in a small frying pan/skillet over medium-high heat and fry the banana flower for 5–6 minutes until crispy. Drain on paper towels.

Heat the oil in a large pan or wok, and gently fry the curry paste. Add the stock or water, vegan fish sauce and brown sugar. Bring to the boil, add the lotus root and squash, and simmer for 7–8 minutes.

Then add the green beans, simmer for another 2–3 minutes, then add the coconut milk and more stock if needed; it should be a soupy consistency. Season with salt to taste, bring back to the boil, then remove from the heat. Stir in the Chinese leaf until nicely wilted.

Fill a bowl or pan with boiling water and blanch the noodles for a few seconds so they are nice and hot. Drain well and place a handful in each bowl. Ladle the curry broth on top. Drizzle with a little chilli/chili oil (if using) and scatter with chopped peanuts (if using) and fried banana flower.

MISO DAUPHINOISE DUMPLINGS *with lime and ginger-glazed black beans*

I made this recipe as part of a trio of dumplings for my final showstopper round in MasterChef. John and Gregg both loved this dumpling, describing the filling as 'meltingly good'. Gregg said the only issue was that I should have made a huge plate of them! Miso is a fabulous ingredient for the vegan cook, and makes a great basis for noodle soups or smothered on a buttery soft aubergine/eggplant, a la Nanban. Patience is the key to achieving the sublime quality to the filling, ensuring that the potato is given enough time to get as soft as mash.

This recipe makes four large dumplings, which can serve four as a small appetizer, or go with Gregg's suggestion and double the quantities to make a big plateful!

TO MAKE THE BLACK BEANS

2 tablespoons light soy or aminos
100 g/½ cup unrefined sugar
freshly squeezed juice of 1 lime
1 tablespoon ginger-preserved
   black beans (or use plain
   preserved and add a small thumb
   of chopped ginger)

TO MAKE THE DUMPLINGS

4 large floury potatoes, such as
   Maris Piper or Yukon Gold
   (or use sweet potato, if you like)
3 tablespoons white miso paste
240 ml/1 cup soy or cashew cream,
   pouring consistency (see page 12)
¼ teaspoon rock salt
¼ teaspoon white pepper
8 sheets of small Vietnamese rice
   papers, about 15 cm/6 inches
1.5–2 litres/6¼–8½ cups vegetable
   stock

*small baking dish, lined with baking
   parchment*
10-cm/4-inch round cookie cutter

SERVES 4

To make the glazed black beans, put all the ingredients in a small pan except the black beans, and bring to a simmer until the liquid is reduced by half. Add the black beans to coat with the glaze. Set aside until later.

Preheat the oven to 180°C (350°F) Gas 4.

To prepare the miso potato dauphinoise, layer the potatoes in the lined baking dish, making several layers to fill the dish.

Mix together the miso paste, cream, salt and white pepper, and pour over the potatoes. Press the potatoes down into the liquid, leave for 10 minutes, and then press down again. Cover with foil and bake in the preheated oven for 45 minutes (halve the cooking time for sweet potatoes), then remove the foil and bake for another 10–15 minutes until the potatoes are fork-soft and golden brown on top. Set aside to cool.

When cooled, cut out four rounds of the potato with the cutter.

Prepare one dumpling at a time. Soak the rice paper in boiling hot water for 10 seconds, then lay a disc of dauphinoise on the paper. Top with another soaked sheet of rice paper. Then, using your hands, bring up the sides of the paper and squeeze together with the top sheet to seal the dumpling, creating a frilly collar. Place the dumplings in the prepared baking dish, and add enough of the vegetable stock to come about halfway up the sides of the dumplings.

Bake for 10–12 minutes in the preheated oven until the upper part of the dumplings are nicely crisped. When they are ready, use a spatula to lift the dumplings carefully out of the dish and place them gently on paper towels to drain.

To serve, place the dumplings on a plate or platter and drizzle with some of the glaze. Scatter a few glazed black beans around and serve immediately.

NANBAN'S VEGAN RAMEN
with shio koji tofu

I'm no expert on ramen, except knowing that the basis of this famously comforting Japanese noodle soup is nearly always bone broth. This sublime vegan recipe was created by Tim Anderson, who beat me to the MasterChef win with his exceptional Japanese and fusion cooking skills, now realised in the form of his Michelin-rated ramen bar in Brixton, Nanban. You might need to visit a Japanese grocery or an online supplier.

TO MAKE THE MUSHROOM DASHI
400 ml/scant 1¾ cups water
50 g/2 oz. kombu
50 g/2 oz. shiitake
50 g/2 oz. porcini
225 ml/scant 1 cup shoyu
70 ml/4½ tablespoons mirin

TO MAKE THE BRAISED DAIKON/MOOLI
½ daikon/mooli, peeled and cut into 13 mm/½ inch thick rounds
250 ml/1 cup water
75 ml/5 tablespoons shoyu
25 ml/1½ tablespoons sake

TO MAKE THE NORI DRESSING
23 g/1 oz. aonori (green laver)
450 ml/scant 2 cups vegetable oil

TO MAKE THE SHIO KOJI TOFU
200 ml/scant 1 cup sake
200 g/7 oz. shio koji
220 g/7½ oz. firm tofu, cut into pieces
1 tablespoon plain/all-purpose flour
1 tablespoon potato flour
¼ teaspoon salt
¼ teaspoon white pepper
500 ml/2 cups sunflower or vegetable oil, for frying

TO MAKE THE RAMEN
260 g/9 oz. soba noodles
200 g/7 oz. Chinese leaves
handful of enoki mushrooms, cleaned
2–3 spring onions/scallions, finely sliced at an angle
¼ teaspoon sesame seeds, lightly toasted
4 g/a pinch of ito kiri togarashi (dried chilli strands, optional)

SERVES 4–5

To make the mushroom dashi, combine the water, kombu, shiitake and porcini in a large pan. Slowly bring to a simmer over low-medium heat. It is very important not to let the dashi boil. When it barely starts to bubble, remove the pan from the heat and leave to infuse for 30 minutes, stirring frequently to ensure all the mushrooms are introduced to the liquid. Pass the dashi through a fine sieve/strainer and season with the shoyu and mirin.

Put the daikon/mooli in a saucepan and cover with the water. Add the shoyu and sake, and part-cover with a lid. Bring to the boil, then simmer over medium heat for 15 minutes until you can push a chopstick through the disc with little effort.

To make the dressing, blend together the aonori and oil until completely smooth and silky. Allow to settle slightly, then pass through a fine sieve/strainer.

To make the shio koji tofu, mix together the sake and shio koji in a large bowl. Add the tofu pieces and marinate for at least 4 hours or overnight.

Mix together the flours, salt and pepper. Heat the oil in a pan over medium-high heat. Once sizzling (a small piece of tofu should sizzle immediately but not burn), dredge the marinated tofu in the seasoned flour and fry for 7–9 minutes until golden and crisp.

Cook the noodles according to the packet instructions. Blanch the Chinese leaf to tenderize slightly. Divide the noodles between the serving bowls, pour in the dashi, add the Chinese leaves and tofu pieces. Slice the daikon/mooli discs in half and add along with the enoki mushrooms, spring onions/scallions, a drizzle of nori oil, sesame seeds and ito kiri togarashi, if you like.

SINIGAG
Filipino breakfast rice

I came across this super easy recipe during one of my many West Coast fusion brunches. Fusion brunch is almost a culinary art form down the West Coast of America. I have never been to the Philippines and it's definitely on my bucket list, if only to eat more of this highly addictive rice. Traditionally the rice is served with fried eggs, and maybe a sweet roll and some kind of pickled vegetable. I think it makes a brilliant foil for almost anything. Don't be intimidated by the quantity of garlic. Serve with slices of buttery soft avocado and pickled vegetables for breakfast, lunch or a light dinner.

120 ml/½ cup cider vinegar
¼ teaspoon dried chilli flakes/
hot red pepper flakes
14 garlic cloves, crushed and
chopped
½–1 teaspoon rock salt, to taste
½ teaspoon ground black pepper
1–2 tablespoons coconut oil
300 g/generous 2½ cups cooked
basmati rice, cooled, preferably
overnight
2 spring onions/scallions, finely
sliced
pickled vegetables, to serve
(optional, see page 135)
1 large avocado, sliced, to serve

SERVES 2

In a small bowl, mix together the vinegar, dried chilli flakes/hot red pepper flakes, 1 tablespoon of the crushed garlic, and the salt and pepper. Stir well and set aside.

Heat the coconut oil in a large frying pan/skillet or wok, over medium-high heat. Add the remaining garlic and fry until golden brown. Tip the garlic onto a plate and return the pan to the heat.

Add the rice and fry over high heat, breaking up any pieces and tossing well for about 8–10 minutes. You want some of the rice to be a little crispy. Add the cooked garlic, keeping back a spoonful for garnishing. Mix well.

Season with more salt, to taste, and transfer to a serving platter. Top with avocado slices and scatter with spring onions/scallions and the reserved fried garlic. Serve with pickled vegetables and the spicy vinegar sauce on the side.

SUAN LA FEN
Sichuan hot and sour sweet potato noodles

This lip-tingling noodle soup stopped me in my tracks the first time I ordered it, in a vegan Sichuan restaurant in Berlin. Served on street corners all over Sichuan China, I've not been able to find it on any menu in the UK. Once I figured out how easy it is to prepare, I soon realised I could knock up this comforting noodle soup in under 15 minutes in my own kitchen. Definitely a comfort recipe worth sharing!

TO MAKE THE SEASONING MIX
2 teaspoons Sichuan peppercorn powder
2 teaspoons Chinese five spice
4 tablespoons Chinese chilli/chili oil
8 tablespoons Chinese black vinegar
4 tablespoons light soy sauce
4 teaspoons sesame oil
1–2 teaspoons salt, to taste

TO MAKE THE NOODLES
3–4 spring onions/scallions, finely sliced
handful of fresh coriander/cilantro
1–2 tablespoons peanut or groundnut oil
5–6 garlic cloves, crushed
300 g/10 oz. sweet potato noodles, soaked in hand-hot water
180 g/6½ oz. pickled mustard leaves, or other preserved vegetable
4 tablespoons roasted red-skinned peanuts

SERVES 6

Mix together the ingredients for the seasoning mix, and divide amongst four serving bowls. Divide half the spring onions/scallions and coriander/cilantro amongst the bowls.

Heat the peanut oil in a heavy-bottomed frying pan/skillet over high heat. Add the crushed garlic, and stir for a few minutes, then divide the hot garlic oil mixture amongst the serving bowls and mix well.

Cook the noodles according to the instructions on the packet, then transfer to the serving bowls, topping up the bowls with a little boiling water and gently stirring. Top the noodles with pickled mustard leaves, roasted peanuts and the remaining chopped spring onions/scallions and coriander/cilantro.

CRISPY MOCK DUCK *pancakes*

Another treat from our childhood birthday trips to the local Chinese restaurant was shredded duck with pancakes and hoisin sauce. With a few little tricks, it's super simple to make a vegan version of this dish. You can also use this 'duck' in a warm salad or as a stuffing with some vermicelli noodles in a spring roll. You can buy canned gluten mock duck from a Chinese supermarket, and sometimes they have a frozen version too. The key is to empty the contents of the can into a sieve/strainer and rinse well with warm water, using your hand to rub off any excess brine and squeeze out the water.

280-g/10-oz. can gluten mock duck, well rinsed
4 tablespoons hoisin sauce (see below or use readymade)
6 spring onions/scallions, trimmed
½ cucumber
10 Chinese-style pancakes, frozen
2 tablespoons plum sauce (optional)

TO MAKE THE HOISIN SAUCE
4 tablespoons agave syrup
2 tablespoons black bean paste
1 tablespoon garlic paste or powder
1 tablespoon Shaoxing rice wine
3 tablespoons water
2 tablespoons dark soy sauce
½ teaspoon Chinese five spice
2 teaspoons toasted sesame oil
¼ teaspoon Sriracha (or use a pinch of chilli/chili powder)

baking sheet, oiled
steamer basket

SERVES 2–3

Preheat the oven to 180°C (350°F) Gas 4.

To make the hoisin sauce, place all the ingredients into a small pan and bring to a simmer. Cook for about 4–5 minutes until the sauce is thickened and glossy. Cool and pour into sterilized jars, where it will keep for several months in the fridge.

Ensure the mock duck is well rinsed, and then shred it into smaller pieces and strips using your hands. Add 2 tablespoons of the hoisin sauce and mix well with your hands.

Layer the pieces onto the prepared baking sheet and bake in the preheated oven for 20–30 minutes, turning halfway through. Cook until the edges are crispy but not burnt.

To prepare the vegetables, use a large, sharp chef's knife to slice the spring onions/scallions in half, then slice each piece lengthways, trying to maintain the shape. Then slice each piece lengthways again, several times, to create spring onion/scallion strips.

Slice the cucumber lengthways and, using a small spoon, scoop out the seeds. Slice each half across the middle, to create four pieces, then cut each piece into thin strips.

Place the steamer basket over a small pan that allows it to sit atop the pan without falling to the bottom. Add about 5 cm/2 inches of water to the pan and bring it to the boil. Add all of the pancakes to the steamer and place it on the pan. Cook the pancakes for about 10–15 minutes until all the pancakes are softened and warm. If you don't have a steamer, you can also place the pancakes, still wrapped, in the microwave for 20 seconds.

To serve, add the remaining hoisin and the plum sauce (if using) into two little pots, alongside the shredded vegetables, steamed pancakes and crispy mock duck. To fill the pancake, spread either hoisin or plum sauce onto the pancake, add a couple of pinches of shredded vegetables and a spoonful of mock duck. Wrap, roll and eat immediately.

JAYK CHIEN
Cambodian-style fried banana

We had been sedately floating about on the river in our little skippered boat. Barely a handful of tourists were around, mostly travelling down from Laos, after crossing overland into Cambodia. Kratie makes a good stop off on the way to Phnom Penh. Roads can be hard-going in Cambodia. They can be unsurfaced featuring giant potholes and thick red dust that turns to deep sticky mud in the rains – we once got stuck for 3 hours in a vehicle knee-deep in mud and had to be pulled out by a digger. Or there's the US-funded tarmacked roads, where less-than-well-serviced vehicles (and drivers) travel at bump-free high speeds, dodging startled horses and their carts. The accident rate is much higher on these roads I'm told. Kratie is a welcome break from the road, with an abundance of cafés and street food, and architecture that strongly echoes Cambodia's former grandeur.

In the riverside village, cooking smells emanated freely from the open kitchen spaces, located underneath the stilted wooden houses. Just a table, a burner and a wok on the go. The latest batch of tourists (us included) clambered out of their boats, and there was a lady with a basket of sweet-smelling fried goodies. Sitting down to watch the glowing Mekong sunset, I scribbled in my little notebook just simply, sesame banana coconut tempura. I wasn't about to miss a trick there.

2 ripe bananas, sliced lengthways and cut into 5-cm/2-inch pieces
sunflower oil, for frying

TO MAKE THE PASSIONFRUIT SYRUP
1 tablespoon water
1 tablespoon caster/superfine sugar
pulp of 2–3 passionfruit

TO MAKE THE BATTER
125 g/generous 1 cup plain/all-purpose flour
80 g/generous ¾ cup cornflour/cornstarch
1 teaspoon bicarbonate of soda/baking soda
1 teaspoon black sesame seeds
½ teaspoon salt
1 tablespoon caster/superfine sugar
½ 400-ml/14-oz. can coconut milk
150 ml/⅔ cup sparkling/soda water

SERVES 3–4

To make the syrup, add the water, sugar and passionfruit pulp to a small pan. Bring to the boil and simmer for 20–30 minutes until reduced and syrupy. Set aside to cool, then strain into a jug/pitcher to remove the passionfruit seeds.

Mix together all the dry ingredients for the batter in a large bowl. Put the coconut milk in a small bowl and mix well to ensure the water and cream are fully combined. Add the sparkling/soda water to the coconut milk and tip into the large bowl of dry ingredients and combine to make a thick batter.

Heat the oil in a wok over medium-high heat until a drop of the batter sizzles but doesn't burn. Once sizzling, dip the banana pieces in the batter and deep-fry, in batches of 3–4, for 8–10 minutes, turning often to ensure they are golden brown all over. Drain on paper towels, then place on a baking sheet in a low oven to keep warm.

When ready to serve, place a few pieces on each plate, add a scoop of strawberry ripple ice-cream (see page 58) and drizzle with the passionfruit syrup.

PINEAPPLE AND CARDAMOM *upside-down cake*

I was about 8 years old when I made my very first pineapple upside-down cake. I followed the recipe from one of my mum's '70s cookery books. I even made her buy the glacé/candied cherries so it would look like the picture. This is like a grown-up version of those childhood memories.

I created this recipe following my stint in the pastry kitchen at Benares, Atul Kochher's famous Mayfair restaurant. As well as creating exquisite Indian food, the team introduced me to the joy of Asian-inspired desserts and pastries. When I admitted I was less keen on traditional Indian desserts, they taught me to take something you love and find an Asian flavour that works well with it. If you're not a cake eater, you could simply poach the pineapple with the cardamom and serve with a scoop of vegan ice-cream. Either way, pineapple and cardamom is a delicious combo however you serve it. It's important to use the right amount of cardamom, as it can taste soapy if you add too much.

1 fresh pineapple (or 300 g/10½ oz. canned pineapple), cut into rings or pieces
1½ tablespoons coconut oil
160 g/generous ¾ cup caster/superfine sugar
225 g/1¾ cups self-raising/self-rising flour
125 g/4 oz. vegan margarine
80 ml/⅓ cup vegan or soy milk
2 flax 'eggs' (see page 15) or egg replacer
1 teaspoon baking powder
1 teaspoon pure vanilla extract
10 green cardamoms, shelled and seeds removed

20-cm/8-inch cake pan, lined

SERVES 6–8

Preheat the oven to 170°C (325°F) Gas 3.

Soften the coconut oil and rub 20 g/1½ tablespoons of the sugar into it. Rub this mixture around the bottom of the lined cake pan and halfway up the sides. Place the pineapple slices across the bottom of the lined cake pan. Set aside.

Grind the cardamom seeds to a powder with a pestle and mortar. Then sift the ground cardamom into a bowl along with the remaining ingredients and whisk together with an electric hand-held whisk.

Pour the mixture into the cake pan and place in the preheated oven for 50–60 minutes, until the cake is evenly risen and a skewer inserted into the centre of the cake comes out clean.

Allow the cake to cool in the pan for 15 minutes before turning out onto a wire rack to cool completely.

CHAI-SPICED RICE PUDDING *with ginger cookies*

I didn't fall in love with masala chai (Indian spiced tea) the first time I drank it, but everywhere we stopped across India and Sri Lanka, there was always a chai-wallah (chai is simply the name for tea and wallah is the seller). After a few months, I found myself hankering for this fragrant and sweet pick-me-up. Being woken by the chai-wallah's calls on the overnight train from Varanasi has long stuck in my memory, and my husband and I still call out to each other 'chai-di-chai' if we're making a brew. I first made this dessert in the early rounds of MasterChef, after I had the pudding foisted upon me when we were asked to cook for previous winners and finalists.

TO MAKE THE CHAI SPICE MIX

2 teaspoons ground ginger (use slices of fresh if you are making tea)

¼ teaspoon ground cinnamon (use 1 large piece of cassia bark or cinnamon stick for tea)

4–5 green cardamom pods, seeds removed and crushed

1 teaspoon ground fennel (use fennel seeds if making tea)

pinch of ground black pepper

2 cloves (optional)

TO MAKE THE PUDDING

100 g/3½ oz. Arborio rice

seeds from 1 vanilla pod/bean

400-ml/14-oz. can coconut milk

350 ml/1½ cups almond, soy, oat or rice milk, plus extra if needed

150 ml/⅔ cup almond or soy cream, plus extra if needed

pinch of freshly grated nutmeg

3 tablespoons brown sugar

TO MAKE THE GINGER BISCUITS

150 g/generous 1 cup self-raising/self-rising flour, plus extra if needed

½ teaspoon bicarbonate of soda/baking soda

2 teaspoons ground ginger

40 g/1½ oz. stem ginger, finely chopped

1 teaspoon ground cinnamon

2 teaspoons caster/superfine sugar

50 g/2 oz. vegan margarine

2 tablespoons golden/light corn syrup

TO MAKE THE MANGO COULIS

1 ripe mango, peeled, stone/pit removed and flesh cubed

TO SERVE

toasted pistachios

2 baking sheets, oiled

SERVES 4–6

Preheat the oven to 190°C (375°F) Gas 5.

Gently toast all the spices for the chai spice mix in a dry frying pan/skillet until the aroma is released.

To make the pudding, place the rice, the seeds of the vanilla pod/bean, the coconut milk, almond milk, almond cream and nutmeg in a large, deep pan. Bring to a gentle boil and add the toasted spices. Simmer for 40–45 minutes, stirring occasionally, adding more cream or milk if needed – the rice should retain a little bite. Sweeten with the brown sugar.

Meanwhile, make the biscuits. Mix all the dry ingredients together in a bowl. In a small pan, gently melt the margarine and syrup together. Pour the melted mixture into the bowl and mix well with the dry ingredients to form a soft and pliable dough. Add more flour if necessary, so that the dough is not too sticky. Roll the dough into small balls.

Flatten the dough balls slightly and place onto the oiled baking sheets, leaving space between each as the mixture will spread as it cooks. Bake in the preheated oven for 10–15 minutes, or until golden. Allow to firm up slightly on the baking sheets, then transfer to a wire rack to cool completely.

For the coulis, put the mango pieces into a small pan with a splash of water and heat gently until very soft. Blend in a food processor or push through a sieve/strainer to make a smooth coulis.

To serve, fill a ramekin with rice pudding and add a swirl of mango coulis. Serve with ginger cookies on the side and sprinkle with the toasted pistachios.

AMERICANA

STATESIDE DINING FOR HUNGRY VEGANS

AMERICANA

We let our teenage twins take charge of the last big trip. With their final year of high school drawing to an end, and hopes of university looming on the horizon, we knew this would probably be one of the last times they would travel with us for an extended period. Like many British teenagers they are fascinated with North American culture. So we planned a route, where I would meet my old travel buddy Maya in Vancouver, Canada, and spend almost a month travelling down the West Coast to LA to meet up with my family. From here we headed further south to San Diego together, then across the southern states to Austin, Texas, and ending with a road trip from New Orleans to New York City. Whenever I told someone of our plans, they usually responded with 'But what will you eat – there's no vegan food in the southern states?'. We've lived off peanut butter and crackers before on our travels so I wasn't worried. It's not like it's the Tibetan plateau.

Cheap, accessible food in North America is very meat-driven. There is no doubt about that. I was actually very surprised to see that mainstream fast food places like McDonalds or Subway don't offer a vegan patty as they do in the UK. No great loss for the vegan food scene, but an observation nonetheless. Perhaps it's because vegans and veggies have so many choices in North America. Why would anyone settle for a vegan patty? For the record, I always take a browse in McDonalds in whichever country I'm visiting as it's a brilliant example of globalization, whatever your politics. I very rarely eat there unless I have to. I once ate noodles in a Maccy Ds in Indonesia. Just because I could. They weren't as bad I was expecting.

The rise of burger culture in the UK has been something I've struggled with during the last five years, as restaurant menus have started to turn this fast food into more gourmet offerings, with very little room for manoeuvre in terms of vegan food, unless a mushy bean patty is your thing. I've lost count of the number of street food events where I've been forced to pitch my food trailer, Barbarella, next to some dastardly burger van, and spend several days repeating, 'No, I don't sell burgers'.

California was a foodie eye-opener on many counts. Not least because of the creative vegan burger culture, from street food parks and even vegan drive-thru's to high-end restaurants serving vegan burgers that are barely distinguishable from their meaty counterparts.

From left to right: Big Sur, California; retro motel in Austin, Texas; farmer's stall selling organic produce; Redwood Forest, Humboldt; San Francisco street food truck.

You can often find good, hearty vegan food where students congregate, and in more offbeat or bohemian areas, like Oakland in San Fran, Bywater in New Orleans or Asheville in North Carolina. What was different was the extent of mid- and high-end vegan food offerings. And the unapologetic re-creation of normally meat-based food; vegan ramen shops, ice-cream parlours, burger joints and restaurants serving American classics, but wholly vegan. It was sometimes a shock to the wallet to be paying top prices for plant-based food, but some of this dining was outstanding and it inspired my recipes here.

There were also times when it felt like vegan food had been gentrified. In the same way developers moved into the slum areas of cities turning previously shunned housing stock into sought-after pads, we ate in restaurants in Portland, LA, New Orleans and New York that showcased vegan food as part of a lifestyle that can require substantial funding.

My first shopping expedition in America's vegan and health food mecca, Wholefoods, blew a melon-sized hole in my wallet. On one hand, it was wonderful to see the range of incredible vegan food available, but on the other, it often felt like elitist consumption, a world away from our experiences of eating in Asia.

There were exceptions. Northern California is predominantly rural, and I enjoyed several stops at a farmer's roadside stall. An impromptu picnic of giant sweet tomatoes, fat creamy avocados and juicy melon was wholly satisfying, and as cheap as any dhaba-café stop in India.

Our experience of roadside stops across the southern US states were sometimes a bit grim for a vegetarian, let alone a vegan. Fortunately we could stock up with imaginative car-picnics, and accommodating staff at roadside cafes would often make us something off-menu, usually involving waffles or sammies. We loved these stops, not so much for the food, but for the interesting glimpses into American culture and everyday life. Asheville, North Carolina, also surprised us with its hipster vibes. We had been snaking our way through the Great Smoky Mountains after whitewater rafting down the Ocoee river, and we were not expecting to find vegan buffalo wings and kombucha.

This section of recipes includes a variety of Canadian- and American-inspired dishes, the comforting and the nourishing, and many of which will convince even the most carnivorous of diners to try some vegan eating.

TOFINO TRINI DOUBLE
The ultimate Trinidadian street food

British Colombia is the kind of place where you can find yourself eating Japanese-Italian fusion in downtown Vancouver and Trinidadian food in Tofino, a laid-back surf town on Vancouver Island's west coast. Trinidadian bara is lighter than Indian puri bread.

TO MAKE THE BARA

7 g/¼ oz. fast-action dried yeast

¼ teaspoon brown sugar

250 ml/1 cup lukewarm water

420 g/scant 3¼ cups plain/all-purpose flour

1 teaspoon ground turmeric

½ tablespoon baking powder

1 teaspoon salt

1 tablespoon sunflower oil, plus extra for oiling the surface

pomace or sunflower oil, for frying

TO MAKE THE TAMARIND SAUCE

200 g/7 oz. soft/wet tamarind, soaked in 500 ml/2 cups boiling water

1 tablespoon brown sugar

TO MAKE THE CHICKPEA CURRY

1 tablespoon coconut oil

1 small onion, finely chopped

2 garlic cloves, crushed

1 teaspoon medium curry powder

1 teaspoon ground turmeric

1 teaspoon cumin seeds, lightly toasted

1 teaspoon garam masala

3–4 tablespoons water

2 x 400-g/14-oz. cans of chickpeas/garbanzo beans

1 teaspoon salt, to taste

½ teaspoon white pepper

handful of freshly chopped coriander/cilantro

2 teaspoons bicarbonate of soda/baking soda

TO SERVE

drizzle of hot sauce

SERVES 4

Mix the yeast, sugar and 50 ml/3½ tablespoons of the water. Leave until frothy; 10–15 minutes. Mix the remaining dry ingredients in a large bowl, add the yeast mix and remaining water. Knead to a smooth dough; 5–10 minutes. Coat with the oil, cover with a damp kitchen towel and let rest in a warm place for 1 hour.

Punch down the dough and knead again briefly. Lightly oil the work surface and roll the dough into 8–10 small balls, about 5 cm/2 inches in diameter.

Place a wok or deep frying pan/skillet over medium-high heat with 5 cm/2 inches of oil for frying. Test the temperature with a pinch of dough; it should sizzle and rise to the top, but not burn.

Flatten each ball to make a 10–12-cm/4–5-inch round. Fry each round in the hot oil for 20–30 seconds on each side. Drain on paper towels, and keep warm in a low oven while you fry the remaining bara.

To make the tamarind sauce, mix the soaking tamarind well using your hands, then push through a sieve/strainer. Add 4 tablespoons of the pulp to a small pan with the brown sugar and a splash of water. Bring to a simmer, taste and add more sugar if needed.

To make the chickpea curry, heat the coconut oil in a pan over medium heat and fry the onion for 10–15 minutes until translucent. Add the garlic and cook for 2–3 minutes. In a small jug/cup, mix the curry powder, ground cumin and garam masala with the water, then add to the onions and cook until the curry paste is almost dry. Add the chickpeas/garbanzo beans and enough water to cover. Stir well and bring to the boil. Simmer gently for 15–20 minutes, then season to taste. Lightly mash the chickpeas slightly, add the coriander/cilantro and stir. Serve atop the warm bara with a drizzle of tamarind sauce and hot sauce.

Poutine is a fast-food comfort dish originating from Quebec, Canada. It's essentially crispy fries smothered in gravy and sprinkled with cheese curds, not dissimilar to Indian paneer. Hence where this idea came from.

Gravy on fries is certainly nothing new for a Mancunian or indeed any northerner; it's a standard item on our chippy menus. The Canadian-style curd has an almost squeaky rubbery quality, so vegan cheese makes a great substitute. The gravy is a rich butter masala-style sauce, which can be used as the basis for a delicious 'butter masala'-style curry, too.

PUNJABI POUTINE
An Indian twist on the Canadian classic

TO MAKE THE SPICED 'CHEESE'
200 g/7 oz. Violife mozzarella-style vegan cheese
4 garlic cloves, minced
1 teaspoon ground ginger
¼ teaspoon chilli/chili powder
¼ teaspoon ground turmeric
1 teaspoon garam masala, lightly toasted
¼ teaspoon salt

TO MAKE THE BUTTER MASALA GRAVY
50 ml/3½ tablespoons vegetable oil or ghee
4–5 cardamom pods, crushed
5-cm/2-inch piece of cassia bark or cinnamon
4 cloves
1 large onion, finely chopped
5-cm/2-inch thumb of ginger, finely chopped
2–4 green chillies/chiles, to taste, cut lengthways

2½ teaspoons mild paprika
½–1 teaspoon chilli/chili powder, to taste
1 teaspoon garam masala
1 teaspoon ground coriander
½ teaspoon fenugreek powder
4 tablespoons tomato purée/paste
2 tablespoons agave syrup or honey
300 ml/1¼ cups water
120 ml/½ cup soy or almond cream
1 teaspoon salt
handful of fresh coriander/cilantro

TO MAKE THE MASALA FRIES
500 g/1 lb. 2 oz. russet, or Maris Piper or Yukon Gold potatoes, with skins on, washed
about 1 litre/4¼ cups sunflower oil, for deep-frying
big pinch of flaked salt

baking sheet, lightly oiled

SERVES 2–3

Preheat the oven to 200°C (400°F) Gas 6.

Cut the cheese into 1-cm/⅜-inch cubes. Mix together the garlic, ginger, chilli/chili powder, turmeric, garam masala and salt in a bowl. Add the cheese, mix well and set aside for 30 minutes.

For the butter masala gravy, heat the vegetable oil in a large pan and add the cardamom, cassia bark and cloves. Gently fry until the aroma is released, then add the onion. Fry gently until the onion is transluscent and starting to turn golden. Remove the whole spices. Add the ginger, chillies/chiles, paprika, chilli/chili powder, ground coriander, garam masala and fenugreek powder to the large pan, and fry gently for 2 minutes. Then add the tomato purée/paste, agave syrup and water. Bring to a simmer and season to taste with salt and more syrup if needed. Simmer gently for 10–15 minutes, then add the cream. Bring back to a simmer, then remove from the heat. This sauce can simply be reheated as needed.

To make the fries, slice the potatoes into 5 mm–1 cm/¼-⅜ inch wide sticks, French fries-style. Heat the oil for deep-frying in a large deep pan or wok over medium heat. The oil needs to be hot enough for blanching on the first frying, around 140°C/280°F. Fry the fries for about 8–10 minutes, then allow to drain on paper towels. Increase the oil temperature to 180°C/350°F and fry the fries for a second time until golden and crispy. Drain on clean paper towels. Repeat in batches, taking care not to crowd the pan. Sprinkle the fries with salt just before serving.

Lay the marinated cheese pieces on the prepared baking sheet and bake in the preheated oven for 6-7 minutes, until gooey and softened. Fill a serving bowl with big handful of fries, pour over the masala sauce and spoon the spiced cheese over the top. Serve immediately.

BBQ ARTICHOKES *with ranch-style dressing*

Driving down the coast of Northern California, with its meandering routes through ancient redwood forests was one of the high points of our journey. Portland, Oregon, had spoiled me with outstanding vegan food, so my options for eating as we made our way down the coast started to appear more limited. We had been side-tracked for hours in the Humboldt Redwoods State Park, hugging trees and standing in awe of these ancient giants. When we stopped for food at a smokehouse and BBQ joint my expectations were fairly low and I prepared myself for ordering fries. And then there they were. Beautifully plump and spiky globe artichokes, smoking away on their own barbeque. I knew immediately they would be delicious and indeed they were.

TO MAKE THE RANCH-STYLE DRESSING
60 g/½ cup cashews, soaked in cold water for 2 hours
120 g/1 cup macadamia nuts (or more cashews, if you prefer)
3 tablespoons freshly squeezed lemon juice
3–4 garlic cloves
1 large celery stick
1 teaspoon rock salt, to taste
2 teaspoons onion powder
150 ml/⅔ cup water, plus extra if needed
2 tablespoons freshly chopped dill

TO MAKE THE BBQ ARTICHOKES
6 weighty globe artichokes
1 lemon, halved
large handful of wood smoking chips (or 1–2 teaspoons smoked essence mixed with a little vegetable oil)

TO SERVE
lemon wedges

SERVES 6

To prepare the dressing, blend together all the ingredients except the dill. Add more water if you prefer a thinner dip. Blend until completely smooth. Then mix in the fresh dill and check the seasoning. Add more salt to taste. This dip will keep for up to 1 week in the fridge.

Slice the artichokes in half using a very sharp, large knife, trimming any excess stem away, too. Using a small paring knife, trim away the hairy choke, just above the heart. Take care not to remove the fleshy heart. Some of the inner leaves will also come away, leaving the exposed heart surrounded by layers of larger leaves. Rub the artichoke insides with the lemon half, to ensure it doesn't start browning immediately.

Place a large pot filled with water over high heat. Squeeze in the juice of the remaining lemon half, bring to the boil, then add the artichoke hearts. Simmer for 30–40 minutes until tender. Drain and leave to cool.

Lay out a sheet of foil and place a large handful of smoking chips in the middle, forming them into a little bed. Wrap the foil around the chips to make a 12.5-cm/5-inch circle, and place in the bottom of a large metal pan that has a lid (I have an old metal pan which I keep for smoking, and store in the shed). Carefully stab a few holes in the top of the foil. Place a metal steamer tray on top of the foil and then lay the artichokes on top. Try to ensure the hearts are well exposed and not covering each other.

Place over medium-high heat with the lid on, and heat until the chips start to smoke. You can peep to check, but don't let the smoke out. Once the chips are nicely smoking, remove from the heat and allow to smoke for 20–30 minutes. Alternatively, you can mix together the smoked essence with some vegetable oil and brush on the artichoke hearts before searing or grilling on your barbecue/outdoor grill.

Just before serving, brush the artichokes with a little oil and place a griddle pan over high heat. Sear on one side only for 6–8 minutes, then serve immediately with the ranch-style dip and a wedge of lemon.

KOREAN-STYLE *cauliflower wings*

One of the great joys of foodie travel is when you eat something delicious in a place you weren't expecting. I'm talking about French food in Laos, Trinidadian food in Tofino, Vietnamese food in Vancouver and Korean food in San Francisco. Nearly every country or region has historical influences on their food culture. British culture has adopted Indian subcontinent food like a favoured sibling.

Travelling down the Pacific Coast gave me opportunities for eating beyond my normal experiences in Europe. Of course, we have Korean and Vietnamese food in the UK, but in Manchester, it's few and far between, and the good stuff even rarer.

And often far from the food culture fusion we experienced in Canada and America, which seemed bold and unapologetic with both ideas and flavours.

I served this for a vegan banquet at the Manchester Food and Drink Festival 2016, and it proved to be one of the most popular courses. Adding vodka to the tempura batter makes it exceptionally light and crispy. You could substitute broccoli and other vegetables if you like. Serve on its own as an appetizer, or alongside some sticky rice, 'slaw (see page 192) and extra sauce on the side.

1 cauliflower, cut into 3-cm/1¼-inch florets

120 g/scant 1 cup potato flour

120 g/scant 1 cup plain/all-purpose flour

½ teaspoon baking powder

½ teaspoon fine salt

40 g/4½ tablespoons sesame seeds

50 g/1 cup coconut flakes or coarse desiccated/dried unsweetened shredded coconut

120 ml/½ cup carbonated water, plus extra if needed

120 ml/½ cup vodka

about 600 ml/2½ cups sunflower or pomace oil, for deep-frying

TO MAKE THE KOREAN-STYLE WING SAUCE

2 tablespoons gochujang (Korean chilli/chili paste)

3 garlic cloves, crushed and finely chopped

2.5-cm/1-inch thumb of ginger, finely chopped (or use ½ teaspoon ground ginger)

2 tablespoons light soy sauce

1 tablespoon rice vinegar

3 tablespoons unrefined muscovado or dark brown sugar

1 tablespoon toasted sesame oil

TO SERVE

2 spring onions/scallions, finely sliced at an angle

¼ teaspoon sesame seeds, lightly toasted

SERVES 4–6

First, prepare the wing sauce by combining all the ingredients in a bowl and whisking until smooth and well combined. Add 1–2 tablespoons of water, if needed, so that sauce can be drizzled or poured. Set aside.

Preheat the oven to 200°C (400°F) Gas 6.

Place the cauliflower florets on a baking sheet and roast in the preheated oven for 10–15 minutes until starting to brown and just cooked through. Set aside to cool.

Heat the oil for deep-frying in a wok or deep pan over medium-high heat. Preheat the oven to 160°C (325°F) Gas 3.

In a large mixing bowl, combine the potato flour, flour, baking powder, salt, sesame seeds and coconut flakes, then add the water and vodka, and whisk until a smooth and fairly thin batter forms. Add more water if needed, so it's of a pouring consistency but will just coat the back of a spoon.

Add the cauliflower pieces to the batter, allow excess batter to drip off, and then place gently in the hot oil. Fry the pieces, in batches, for 4–6 minutes, and agitate them so they are golden brown and crispy all over. Drain on paper towels. Keep warm in the oven while you fry the rest of the pieces.

Mix the fried cauliflower pieces with the wing sauce in a large bowl. Serve immediately, with a sprinkle of spring onions/scallions and sesame seeds on top.

BIG BEET BURGER *with beer-battered pickles*

This is a salute to the No-No Burger. I loved almost everything about San Francisco, except for joining a line outside popular restaurants. Sometimes for over an hour. I kept thinking this wouldn't fly at all back home, but then I head to somewhere popular to eat in the UK and apparently it does. Table bookings are becoming a thing of the past, it seems. I don't like this trend. But where I really wanted to eat in San Fran was a new street food park; a dedicated downtown space for street food trucks and the like, with seating and even a covered dining area in a disused yellow school bus.

I had read about No-No burgers, which are considered to be one of the best vegan burgers on the West Coast by some. There's always a danger with such hype, but I was happily impressed by one of the best I've ever tasted (although I've yet to taste the Impossible burger). I don't eat veggie or vegan burgers much as I'm not a fan of the mushy beany type of patty that is popular in the UK. This recipe has been a long time in the making, as I tried to recreate the flavours and textures I loved about the No-No and other great vegan burgers we sampled along the way. This recipe takes a little work, but the patties can be frozen and you can also use the vegan mince for other recipes, such as the marinara vegball sub (see page 174). This patty mixture will make up to eight, so you can freeze four for another time.

TO MAKE THE MINCE
300 g/1¼ cups vital wheat gluten
50 g/1 cup nutritional yeast
2 teaspoons paprika
300 ml/1¼ cups vegetable broth
1 tablespoon liquid smoke
2 garlic cloves, crushed and finely chopped
½ teaspoon yeast extract
2 tablespoons olive or vegetable oil
½ tablespoon dark soy sauce (or 1 tablespoon aminos)

TO FINISH THE PATTY
3 tablespoons coconut oil, plus extra for cooking
100 g/generous ½ cup split peas, soaked overnight

1 onion, finely chopped
2 celery sticks, finely chopped
2 small beetroots/beets, roasted whole, peeled and finely chopped
2 garlic cloves, crushed and finely chopped
1 tablespoon sundried tomatoes, finely chopped
1 teaspoon garlic powder
1 teaspoon paprika
1 teaspoon smoked essence
½ mustard powder
1 tablespoon soy sauce or aminos
½ teaspoon onion powder
½ teaspoon white pepper
1 teaspoon fine rock salt
1 teaspoon ground cumin
1 tablespoon kibbled/crispy fried onions
½ tablespoon freshly squeezed lemon juice

Preheat the oven to 180°C (350°F) Gas 4.

Prepare the mince by mixing together the wheat gluten, nutritional yeast and paprika. In another bowl, mix together the stock, liquid smoke, minced garlic, yeast extract, olive oil and dark soy sauce. Then add the wet mix to the dry mix, and bind together to make a dough. Knead well for 4–5 minutes.

Shape the dough into 4–5 large balls. Tear some foil into large squares and place the dough balls onto a square each. Loosely fold up the sides, creating a loose seal at the top and place in a deep baking pan. Half-fill the pan with hot water and place in the preheated oven for 50–60 minutes until the dough is completely cooked. They will have almost doubled in size. Set aside to cool.

TO MAKE THE BURGER SAUCE

4 tablespoons vegan
    mayonnaise
    (see page 12)
2 tablespoons ketchup
½ teaspoon vinegar
1 tablespoon burger
    relish
½ tablespoon freshly
    chopped dill
1 teaspoon Henderson's
    relish, vegan
    Worcestershire sauce
    or light soy
½ teaspoon yellow
    mustard
¼ teaspoon salt
½ teaspoon agave syrup
    (or ¼ teaspoon sugar)

TO MAKE THE PICKLES

4 large dill pickles
80 g/scant ⅔ cup potato
    flour
80 g/scant ⅔ cup plain/
    all-purpose flour
½ tablespoon Korean red
    pepper powder
1 teaspoon fine salt
330-ml/12-oz. bottle of
    IPA or beer, substitute
    sparkling/soda water
    if you prefer
400 ml/scant 1¾ cups
    sunflower oil, for frying

TO SERVE

4 slices of vegan cheddar-
    style cheese, such as
    Violife 'cheddar'
4 seeded burger rolls
1 battavia lettuce
1 beef tomato, sliced
1 red onion, sliced into
    rings

baking sheet, oiled

SERVES 4

Once cooled, place half the pieces in a food processor and blitz to make a rough-textured mince. Repeat until all the cooked dough is minced. This can be frozen for other uses at this stage.

Heat the coconut oil in a frying pan/skillet and sauté the chopped onion and celery over medium heat for 10–15 minutes until completely translucent and softened. Add the beetroots/beets and sun-dried tomatoes, and cook for a further few minutes.

Place the remaining patty ingredients in a large mixing bowl and add the onion mixture from the pan along with the mince. Using your hands, mix well to make a sticky but firm patty dough. Shape into rounds, approximately 2.5 cm/1 inch deep and 10–12 cm/4–5 inches wide. Place on the oiled baking sheet and cover. Leave in the fridge for 1–2 hours to set, or overnight if possible.

To make the burger sauce, add all the ingredients to a small bowl and mix well. Cover and set aside in the fridge until needed.

To cook the burgers, add 1–2 tablespoons of coconut oil to a large frying pan/skillet and place over low heat. Gently fry the burgers, in batches, for 20–25 minutes, turning occasionally. Meanwhile, preheat the oven to 170°C (340°F) Gas 4. Once the burgers are cooked, place them on a baking sheet in the oven to keep warm, topped with a slice of vegan cheese, if you like. Leave in the oven to melt the cheese.

To prepare the pickles, slice the dill pickles in half lengthways. Mix together the flour, potato flour, red pepper powder and salt in a bowl. Add the beer and mix to form a runny batter that just coats the back of a spoon. Heat the oil for deep-frying in a small, deep pan over medium-high heat. Check the oil is hot enough by dropping a little batter into the pan. If it sizzles and rises, the oil is ready. Carefully dip the pickles into the batter and place into the hot oil. Fry in batches of 3–4, cooking for about 6–7 minutes until golden and crispy. Drain on paper towels.

To serve the burgers, lightly toast the sliced rolls on the inside. Slather the bottom half with 1 tablespoon of burger sauce than add a lettuce leaf or two, followed by a burger patty. Top the burger with a slice of vegan cheese, a slice of tomato and a few onion rings, then top with the top of the roll. Skewer a couple of pickles and push the skewer through the top of the burger. Serve immediately with some fries and extra burger sauce on the side.

MARINARA *vegball sub*

Another bursting-at-the-seams sandwich. You could serve the filling over pasta, but there's something satisfying about this vegan version of the Italian-American classic. A classic marinara sauce tends to include only tomatoes, but I prefer a more substantial vegetable ragù. Serve with plenty of napkins as things will get messy!

TO MAKE THE MARINARA SAUCE

3 tablespoons olive oil
1 onion, finely chopped
4 fat garlic cloves, crushed
1 carrot, peeled and grated
1 celery stick, finely chopped
1 small red (bell) pepper finely chopped
2 400-g/14-oz. cans of Italian whole tomatoes, San Marzano if you really want to push the boat out
½–1 teaspoon rock salt, to taste
½ teaspoon ground black pepper
handful of oregano, roughly chopped (or use ¼ teaspoon dried)
handful of roughly torn basil leaves
200 ml/scant 1 cup water, plus extra if needed

TO MAKE THE VEGBALLS

120 g/⅔ cup split channa dal (split yellow peas), soaked overnight
500 g/1 lb. 2 oz. vegan mince (see page 170, or use readymade TVP mince)
80 g/1 cup dried breadcrumbs
16 g/4 tablespoons nutritional yeast
75 g/1 cup vegan Italian-style hard cheese, grated
handful of freshly chopped parsley
2 tablespoons flax 'egg' (see page 15) or egg replacer
½–1 teaspoon salt, to taste
1 teaspoon ground black pepper
½ teaspoon ground white pepper
3 tablespoons olive oil
1 garlic clove, crushed

FOR THE CASHEW 'CHEESE' SAUCE

120 g/1 cup cashews, soak in water for 3 hours
300 ml/1¼ cups almond milk
9 g/2 tablespoons tapioca flour
4 tablespoons nutritional yeast
1 teaspoon garlic powder
½–1 teaspoon salt, to taste

TO SERVE

4 sub rolls or half-size baguettes
grated vegan Italian-style hard cheese (optional)
handful of freshly torn basil

SERVES 4

For the marinara sauce, heat the olive oil in a heavy-bottomed pan over medium-high heat, and add the onion, garlic, carrot, celery and red (bell) pepper. Fry gently for 10–15 minutes until well softened. Using a potato masher, gently squash all the vegetables to a rough paste. Add the tomatoes and their juice along with the salt, pepper, herbs and water. Bring to the boil and simmer for 45 minutes until thickened. Add more water if necessary, and check the seasoning.

To prepare the vegballs, grind the channa dal in a food processor to make a fine crumb and then transfer to a bowl with the mince, breadcrumbs, nutritional yeast, vegan cheese, parsley, flax 'egg', salt and pepper. Using your hands, mix everything together. Add a little water if needed to make a pliable mixture, and shape into 24–28 3-cm/1¼-inch balls.

Add the olive oil to a large frying pan/skillet and add the crushed garlic clove. Place over high heat and fry until browned, then remove from pan. Add the vegballs in batches to the garlic oil and fry gently over medium heat until browned on all sides (do not crowd the pan). Drain on paper towels. Transfer the balls to the sauce, bring to a simmer, then stir gently.

Drain the soaked cashews and add to a blender with the other ingredients for the cashew cheese sauce. Blitz to a paste, pour into a saucepan and heat gently, stirring until thickened and gooey.

To serve, slice the sub rolls in half, and lightly toast the inside. Lay the lower half on a baking sheet and top with several meatballs and a little marinara sauce. Pour some cashew cheese sauce on top. Place under a hot grill/broiler for 1–2 minutes, if you like. Grate a little vegan cheese on top, scatter over some basil, then top with other half of the roll or baguette.

TEVO'S TEXAN SCRAMBLE
breakfast burrito

If I had stayed in Portland any longer, I would need to take up distance-running to counter that amount of good eating. Stumptown, as it's colloquially known, is like coming home for a vegan. I cannot wait to return to Oregon one day, as there's some serious exploring to be done in a state that has everything I love about the magnificently wild Pacific Northwest region, but with vineyards and a Manc-like creativity and attitude to life.

It was hard to choose between Voodoo's irresistible doughnuts and yet another fine brunch. Breakfast and brunch scrambles are popular everywhere, as is brunch itself. There were nearly always great vegan options too, with scrambled tofu, vegan sausages and 'chorizo'. This recipe is a mash-up between my favourite Portland breakfast scramble and my son's brunch burrito, something he concocted when he first left for university.

8 Charlotte or midi potatoes, skin on, diced into 1.5-cm/½-inch chunks
¼ teaspoon ground turmeric
1 tablespoon olive oil
2 vegan 'chorizo' sausages, sliced
1 small red onion, finely sliced
2 fresh large red chillies/chiles, finely sliced
240 g/8½ oz. firm tofu
16 cherry tomatoes, halved
3–4 spring onions/scallions, finely sliced
1 large soft avocado, stoned/pitted, peeled and sliced
handful of fresh coriander/cilantro
4 large tortilla wraps
1 fresh lime, cut into quarters
2–3 tablespoons hot sauce (optional)

baking sheet, oiled

SERVES 4

Preheat the oven to 190°C (375°F) Gas 5.

Place the potatoes onto the oiled baking sheet, sprinkle with ground turmeric and place in the preheated oven for 20–30 minutes until golden brown and cooked through.

Heat ½ tablespoon of the oil in a large frying pan/skillet and fry the 'chorizo' until starting to brown a little on both sides. Remove from the pan and set aside. To the same pan, add the remaining oil, red onion and red chilli/chile. Fry for a few minutes over medium-high heat, then add the tofu, crumbling it into the pan with your hands. Sauté for a few minutes, then add the potatoes and 'chorizo'. Mix well and cook for a further 3–4 minutes until everything is hot and sizzling. Add the tomatoes and spring onions/scallions, then remove the pan from the heat. Mix well.

Lay the tortillas onto plates, and add a few tablespoonfuls of the mixture to the centre of each wrap. Lay 2–3 slices of avocado on top and finish with a sprinkle of fresh coriander/cilantro and a splash of hot suace, if you like. Fold in the lower side of the wrap, then fold in the sides and roll to make a snug burrito parcel. Serve immediately.

SWEETCORN CHOWDER *with lime and black bean salsa and chilli-spiced arepa biscuits*

Oh, how Americans love their chow-dah! Its original home may be New England, but chowder is a dish that's travelled far and wide around the globe. I wonder if we can call this recipe a chowder at all as it misses out on all that seafood, but sweetcorn is the perfect addition to the creamy and rich potato broth, spiked with punchy salsa and spiced cornmeal biscuits for a satisfying bowl of American-inspired comfort.

TO MAKE THE CHOWDER

4 fresh corn cobs (or use 500 g/1 lb. 2 oz. frozen corn)
1 tablespoon olive oil
1 large leek, sliced lengthways and finely sliced
1 onion, finely chopped
2 celery sticks, finely chopped
2 bay leaves
several sprigs of fresh thyme
2 waxy potatoes, peeled and diced into 1-cm/⅜-inch cubes
500 ml/2 cups vegetable stock
150 ml/⅔ cup almond or soy milk (unsweetened)
50 ml/3½ tablespoons vegan cream
1 tablespoon potato flour or tapioca starch, mixed with water to make a paste
1–2 teaspoons salt, to taste
½ teaspoon ground white pepper
½ teaspoon ground black pepper

TO MAKE THE BLACK BEAN SALSA

200-g/7-oz can of black beans, rinsed and drained
freshly squeezed juice of 1 lime
½ small red onion, finely chopped
1 small red chilli/chile, finely chopped
16 cherry tomatoes, quartered
1 tablespoon freshly chopped coriander/cilantro
½ tablespoon olive oil
salt, to taste

TO MAKE THE AREPA BISCUITS

120 g/generous ¾ cup fine cornmeal/polenta
½–1 teaspoon dried chilli flakes/hot red pepper flakes, to taste
½ teaspoon fine salt
1 teaspoon baking powder
240 ml/1 cup warm water
2 tablespoons olive oil

baking sheet, lined

SERVES 4

Using a sharp knife, carefully slice down the sides of the corn cobs to remove the corn kernels.

Heat the olive oil in a large pan over medium heat and sauté the leek, onion, celery, bay and thyme for 8–10 minutes until translucent and well softened. Add the potatoes and stock and bring to the boil. When the potato is almost cooked, remove from the heat. Remove the bay leaves and thyme stalks. Add the corn to the pan and stir well. Pour half of the mixture into a blender and blitz for a minute, then pour back into the pan. Stir well and add the milk, cream and potato flour. Bring to a simmer for a few minutes, season with the salt and peppers, and set aside.

Combine the salsa ingredients together and mix well, adding a little salt to taste. Set aside.

Preheat the oven to 180°C (350°F) Gas 4.

To make the biscuits, whisk together the cornmeal/polenta, dried chilli flakes/hot red pepper flakes, salt and baking powder in a bowl. Add the water and olive oil, and knead to form a soft dough. Cover with a clean kitchen towel and leave to rest for 5–10 minutes. Once rested, knead again. The dough should have become a little firmer.

Break off a small piece of dough and roll to make a small ball. Then flatten using your thumb, and place on the lined baking sheet. Repeat with the remaining dough, to make approx. 12 biscuits. Place the baking sheet in the preheated oven for 8–10 minutes until the biscuits are golden and cooked.

Serve the chowder in soup bowls and place a spoonful of the black bean salsa in the middle of each bowl. Serve 3–4 arepa biscuits on the side.

CREAMY DREAMY QUESADILLA
with avocado and sweetcorn

My favourite quesadillas are thin and crispy, with an oozy warm filling, drizzled in some hot chipotle sauce. But in my quest to eat less cheese, I'm always on the look out for alternatives. San Diego seemed to have as many Mexican eateries as Manchester has Indian ones. With the southern Californian penchant for all things vegan, together with the most buttery avocados I've ever tasted, there was never a shortage of vegan variations. These quesadillas are even more delicious served alongside a fresh salsa of ripe tomatoes.

TO MAKE THE SALSA
250 g/9 oz. cherry tomatoes, quartered
freshly squeezed juice of ½ lime
½ red onion, finely diced
1–2 jalapeño chillies/chiles, finely chopped
¼–½ teaspoon fine salt, to taste

TO MAKE THE FILLING
200 g/7 oz. fresh, frozen or canned sweetcorn
1–2 tablespoons olive oil
1 shallot, finely chopped
¼ teaspoon ground cumin
¼ teaspoon chilli/chili powder
1 garlic clove, crushed
freshly squeezed juice of ½ lime
½ teaspoon salt
½ teaspoon white pepper
2 ripe avocados, stoned/pitted, peeled and sliced

TO SERVE
1 tablespoon olive or vegetable oil
4 soft 20-cm/8-inch flour tortillas
2–4 tablespoons habanero or other hot sauce, to serve

SERVES 4

Combine all the salsa ingredients in a small bowl. Set aside in the fridge until you are ready to serve.

If using fresh sweetcorn in the filling, blanch it in boiling water for 4–5 minutes until the kernels are soft and ready to eat.

Heat the olive oil in a small frying pan/skillet, add the shallot and sauté for 5–6 minutes until starting to soften. Add the cumin, chilli/chili powder and garlic, and cook for a further 2–3 minutes.

Divide the sweetcorn in half, and roughly mash or blitz one half in food processor to make a rough purée. Add the puréed corn and the remaining whole corn kernels to the frying pan/skillet and mix well. Remove from the heat, add the lime juice, salt and pepper, and mix well so everything is combined. Set aside.

In a small bowl, lightly mash the avocados with a fork. Add a generous tablespoon of avocado onto each tortilla and spread over one half. Then add the sweetcorn mixture and fold the tortilla over to make a semicircle shape.

To serve, heat a splash of the oil in a large frying pan/skillet and place over medium heat. Place the folded tortilla into the pan and cook on each side for a few minutes, until just browning and a little crispy. Remove from the pan and keep warm in a low oven while cooking the remaining quesadillas. When ready to serve, slice each quesadilla in half to make two quarter shapes. Serve with a dollop of tomato salsa and some habanero sauce.

PO-BOY *with NOLA-style jackfruit*

When I told people we were taking a road trip across the southern states of America, many frowned with concerns about what we would eat. Almost famously dedicated to their meat and fish, I wondered if the vegan trend had spread between the two coasts of America. New Orleans did not let us down. Po-Boy is a Louisiana classic; a giant stuffed baguette-style sandwich created in a New Orleans restaurant by the Martin brothers, to feed the poverty stricken men (or poor boys) during the violent streetcar strikes in the late '20s. Its popularity never dwindled and these days they are even serving vegan versions.

TO MAKE THE REMOULADE
1 red (bell) pepper
1 chipotle or jalapeño chilli/chile
2 spring onions/scallions
3 tablespoons vegan mayonnaise (see page 12)
1 teaspoon freshly squeezed lemon or lime juice
2 tablespoons rice vinegar
½ tablespoon smoked paprika
½ teaspoon yellow mustard
2–3 dill pickles, finely chopped

FOR THE FILLING
160 g/scant 1¼ cups plain/all-purpose flour
400-g/14-oz. can green jackfruit, rinsed and drained
2 green tomatoes, thickly sliced (optional, use unripe green Heritage as substitute)
3 flax 'eggs' (see page 15) or egg replacer
about 400 ml/scant 1¾ cups pomace or vegetable oil, for deep-frying

TO MAKE THE CAJUN SPICE POWDER
1 teaspoon fine salt
1 teaspoon garlic powder
1 teaspoon paprika
½ teaspoon ground black pepper
½ teaspoon onion powder
½ teaspoon chilli/chili powder
½ teaspoon dried oregano
½ teaspoon dried thyme
¼ teaspoon dried chilli flakes/hot red pepper flakes

TO SERVE
2 baguettes, halved lengthways
2 spring onions/scallions, finely sliced
hot sauce

baking sheet, lightly oiled

SERVES 4

Preheat the oven to 210°C (410°F) Gas 6.

First prepare the remoulade. Halve the (bell) pepper, remove the core and place on the lightly oiled baking sheet in the hot oven for 10–15 minutes until soft and starting to blacken at the edges. Place the (bell) pepper in a food bag and set aside to cool (this will help the skin to come away from the flesh). Once cooled, peel away and discard the skin.

Put the roasted (bell) pepper in a food processor with the rest of the ingredients for the remoulade, except the pickles. Blitz until smooth and then place in a small bowl. Add the chopped pickles, mix well and set aside in the fridge.

Next, mix together all the spices for the Cajun spice powder.

For the filling, mix 3 teaspoons of the Cajun spice mixture with the flour. Slice the tomatoes into 1 cm/⅜ inch thick slices.

Place a large pan over high heat with the oil for deep-frying, approximately 5 cm/2 inches in depth. Dip the tomatoes and jackfruit pieces into the flax 'eggs' and then coast in the spiced flour mixture. Gently drop the tomatoes and jackfruit into the sizzling oil and fry for a few minutes until golden and crispy. Drain on paper towels.

Slice the baguette, and toast it lightly on the inside. Spread the remoulade over the inside of the bread, lay a lettuce leaf or two inside then add the crispy jackfruit and tomatoes. Sprinkle with sliced spring onions/scallions and serve with some hot sauce on the side.

LOUISIANA-STYLE *BBQ sauce*

The sticky hot rain reminded us of tropical Asia, with Louisiana's steamy backwaters dripping in dense shades of green, and the pulsing sounds of insects and birdlife. Vast drives along monotonous highways, that often felt like eternal bridges across miles of submerged land. It was easy to forget exactly where we were. The sign in the window at the petrol/gas station, that asked customers to please leave their gun in their vehicle, was a stark reminder we were not in California anymore.

People in the southern states love a bit of hot sauce with their food. This made me like them even more. With their almost hypnotic and soothing drawl, people were incredibly warm and welcoming, and not at all phased by our vegetarian tendencies. Delicious hot sauces came in handy for serving alongside numerous styles of beans and greens. This spicy BBQ-style sauce is simple to prepare and can be used as a marinade or dipping sauce. You can make it as spicy as you prefer. It will keep for up to two weeks in the fridge. The 'magic dust' BBQ rub can be used as a dry marinade on any vegetables or even tofu, before roasting or BBQing.

120 ml/½ cup tomato ketchup
30 ml/2 tablespoons cider vinegar
30 ml/2 tablespoons Henderson's relish or vegan Worcestershire sauce
25 g/2 tablespoons unrefined brown sugar
1 tablespoon molasses
1 tablespoon yellow mustard
2 tablespoons hot sauce, such as Tabasco
½ teaspoon ground black pepper
½–1 teaspoon chilli/chili powder, to taste

TO MAKE THE 'MAGIC DUST' BBQ RUB
6 g/1 scant tablespoon paprika
3 g/½ scant tablespoon mustard powder
3 g/½ scant tablespoon Korean red pepper powder
3 g/½ scant tablespoon hot chilli/chili powder
3 g/½ scant tablespoon cayenne pepper
3 g/½ tablespoon ground cumin
3 g/½ scant tablespoon garlic powder
1 teaspoon freshly ground black pepper
1 teaspoon fine salt

MAKES 250 ML/1 CUP

In a small bowl, whisk together the dry 'magic dust' ingredients.

Combine 1 tablespoon of the 'magic dust' with all the other ingredients in a small saucepan. Bring to the boil over medium-high heat, then reduce the heat and simmer for 10–15 minutes until thick and glossy. Transfer to a sterilized jar and keep in the fridge. The remaining dry 'magic dust' mixture can be stored in an airtight spice tub or jar in the cupboard.

MISSISSIPPI MASH
with dirty beans and crispy okra

We arrived in Memphis feeling a little frazzled after a long drive north through Louisiana and into Tennessee. We stretched our legs along the banks of the Mississippi watching the riverboats and slurping ice slushies in the fearsome heat. There had been much family debate about what to visit during our brief stay here. The final vote fell in favour of a visit to the National Civil Rights Museum at the Lorraine Motel, the place where Martin Luther King Jr. was assassinated. We ended our enlightening, emotional and spine-tingling visit in a nearby café where the list of southern-style vegetables filled a 60-cm/2-ft. banner hanging outside. We may be vegetarian but we would not be going hungry.

Vegetarians and vegans have to keep an eye out for unexpected porky bits when ordering American-style beans but we enjoyed lots of meat-free greens and beans, and the Louisiana classic rice and bean dish known as dirty rice. This recipe brings together some of my favourite southern-style veggies on one big comforting plate.

TO MAKE THE DIRTY BEANS
120 g/⅔ cup dried pinto beans
120 g/⅔ cup dried aduki beans
1–2 tablespoons pomace or vegetable oil
1 large onion, diced
2 celery sticks, trimmed and diced
2 garlic cloves, crushed and finely chopped
2 small carrots, peeled and diced
1 green (bell) pepper, seeded and diced
¼ teaspoon chilli/chili powder
1 teaspoon paprika
couple of sprigs of dried thyme
1 bay leaf
1.5 litres/6¼ cups vegetable stock
1 bunch of collard/spring greens or kale, stems removed and roughly chopped

TO MAKE THE MASH
4 tablespoons pomace or light olive oil
1 onion, sliced
2 garlic cloves, crushed and finely chopped (or 1 teaspoon garlic powder)
½–1 teaspoon fine salt, to taste
½ teaspoon white pepper
½ teaspoon black pepper
6 red potatoes, unpeeled, washed and sliced into 5 mm/¼ inch thick discs

TO MAKE THE OKRA
about 400 ml/scant 1¾ cups sunflower oil, for deep-frying
18 okra fingers
250 ml/1 cup soy or other vegan milk
80 ml/⅓ cup vegan cream
250 g/1⅔ cups fine cornmeal/polenta
½ teaspoon fine salt
1 teaspoon ground black pepper

SERVES 4–6

Right: Paddle wheel steamboat on the Mississippi.

First, prepare the beans. Rinse them, then place in a large, deep pan and cover with several litres/quarts of water. Bring to the boil and simmer for 30–40 minutes until just soft. Rinse, drain and set aside.

Heat the oil in a large frying pan/skillet or wok over medium-high heat. Add the onion and celery, then sauté for 10–12 minutes until translucent and softened. Add the garlic, carrots and green (bell) pepper and cook for a further 8–10 minutes. Add the chilli/chili powder, paprika, thyme, bay leaf and stock, and bring to the boil. Turn down the heat and simmer for 10 minutes, then add the beans and greens, and simmer for another 15–20 minutes.

To make the mash, add the oil to a large lidded frying pan/skillet and place over medium-high heat. Fry the sliced onion for 5–6 minutes until it starts to caramelize. Add the garlic, salt and peppers, and stir well. Add the potatoes, mixing well to ensure they are well coated in the onion mixture. Turn down the heat to low and place the lid on the pan. Cook for 20–30 minutes, turning and mixing occasionally.

Once the potatoes start to soften, use a metal spatula to chop into the potato pieces, roughly mashing the mixture by repeatedly chopping it. Once the potatoes are completely soft and roughly mashed, remove from the heat. Adjust the seasoning to taste.

Place a small pan over medium heat and heat the oil for deep-frying. Check the oil is hot enough by dropping a few specks of cornmeal/polenta into it. It should sizzle but not burn. Preheat the oven to 160°C (325°F) Gas 3.

Slice the okra lengthways. Mix the milk and cream in a wide, shallow bowl and put the cornmeal/polenta in another. Dip the okra pieces into the milk mixture then into the cornmeal/polenta. Ensure the okra is well coated with the cornmeal/polenta. Fry the okra, in batches, and then drain on paper towels. Keep warm on a baking sheet in the warm oven. Season with salt and pepper before serving.

To serve, place a few scoopfuls of the mash onto plates or into wide bowls, making a slight well in the middle. Top with several tablespoonfuls of beans and a few pieces of crispy okra. Serve immediately.

THE REUBEN, HONESTLY

Vegan take on a classic NYC deli sandwich

Americans love their sandwiches, or 'sammies'. They are often epic in size and seem to celebrate the no holds barred approach to fillings. For me, the Reuben is one of the ultimate classics for an American sandwich. I was already a vegetarian by the time I reached NYC in my late teens, so when I first wandered into Katz's Deli on 2nd Ave, the only sandwich option for me was a classic egg salad. It was delicious, but still, it was only an egg salad sandwich. I spied the stacked mega-snacks and took in spicy aromas being consumed by meat-eaters and felt a pang of food-envy.

Fast forward 25 years and I'm with my family ordering lunch in a café in Venice, LA. But this is no ordinary café. Café Gratitude is a vegan restaurant serving outstanding food that took us all by surprise,

alongside a few gentle reminders about mindfulness and gratitude. Not in a preachy way. And even if it had been, you'd forgive them because the food was so good. The dish that blew me away was their vegan take on The Reuben called 'Honest'. Slightly salty smoky tempeh with perfectly balanced pickles, and an unusual but delicious quinoa bread. When I returned to the UK, I was very pleased to find that the bread is fairly easy to make, although you could just substitute some good-quality rye bread.

600 g/1 lb. 5 oz. smoked
  tempeh
4 tablespoons sauerkraut
  (see opposite)
4 vegan cheese slices,
  such as Violife

TO MAKE THE BRINE

2 small beetroots/beets
1.5 litres/6¼ cups water
5 cloves, crushed
5-cm/2-inch thumb
  of ginger, sliced
200 g/7 oz. rock salt
1 teaspoon black
  peppercorns
1 teaspoon dried chilli
  flakes/hot red pepper
  flakes
1 teaspoon allspice
¼ teaspoon freshly
  grated nutmeg
1 small cinnamon sticks,
  crushed or broken into
  pieces
1 bay leaf, crumbled

TO MAKE THE QUINOA BREAD

360 g/generous 2 cups
  red quinoa, soaked
  overnight in 1 litre/4¼
  cups water and
  ¼ teaspoon salt
360 ml/1½ cups water
2 tablespoons flax 'egg'
  (see page 15) or egg
  replacer
180 g/generous 1½ cups
  rye flour
1 tablespoon baking
  powder
1 teaspoon sea salt

TO MAKE THE RUB

1 tablespoon coarsely
  ground black pepper
½ tablespoon ground
  coriander
1 teaspoon smoked
  paprika
¼ teaspoon mustard
  powder
¼ teaspoon garlic
  powder
¼ teaspoon onion
  powder
1 teaspoon brown sugar

TO MAKE THE DRESSING

1 tablespoon finely
  chopped onion
6 tablespoons vegan
  mayonnaise
  (see page 12)
2 tablespoons tomato
  ketchup
2 teaspoons horseradish
  sauce
¼–1 teaspoon hot pepper
  sauce, such as Encona,
  to taste
1 teaspoon Henderson's
  relish or vegan
  Worcestershire sauce
pinch of paprika
¼ teaspoon fine rock salt

loaf pan, oiled

SERVES 4

First prepare the brine for the tempeh. Add the peeled and roasted beetroots/beets to a blender with 1 litre/4¼ cups of the water and blitz until completely smooth. Pour into a pan and add the remaining brine ingredients along with the remaining 500 ml/2 cups of water. Bring to a simmer over medium heat. Cook for 8 minutes then remove from the heat and cool slightly.

Slice the tempeh block into four long, equal pieces and lay in a deep dish. Pour over the beetroot/beet brine. Cover and place the dish in the fridge overnight, or even for two nights, if you can wait that long.

Preheat the oven to 180°C (350°F) Gas 4.

Rinse the soaked quinoa and place in a blender with 120 ml/½ cup of the water and the flax 'egg'. Blitz until smooth, then add the remaining water and all the other ingredients to make a thick batter. Pour into the oiled loaf pan and bake in the preheated oven for 50–60 minutes. Remove from the oven and allow to stand for a few minutes before turning onto a wire rack to cool.

When ready, remove the tempeh from the brine. Rinse well and set aside to dry. Mix together the dry rub ingredients in a shallow dish and add the tempeh pieces. Coat in the rub and set aside to marinate for an hour or so.

To make the dressing, use a pestle and mortar to smash the onion into a rough paste. Then add it to the remaining ingredients in a small bowl, and mix well. Cover with clingfilm/plastic wrap and set aside in the fridge.

Preheat the oven to 170°C (340°F) Gas 4.

Place the tempeh pieces on a baking sheet and cover with foil. Place the tray into the preheated oven and cook for 40–45 minutes.

To construct the sandwich, slice the quinoa bread to make eight 1 cm/⅜ inch thick slices. Place the bread under the grill/broiler and lightly toast on one side. Remove four slices and turn the other four over. Lay a vegan cheese slice on each piece and place back under the grill/broiler for a few minutes until melted.

Meanwhile, slice the tempeh into 3 mm/⅛ inch thick slices. Generously slather the dressing onto the half-toasted bread (without the cheese), then lay several slices of tempeh on top. Next add a tablespoon of drained sauerkraut and finally top with the remaining toasted bread, cheese-side down. Repeat to make four sandwiches. Serve immediately.

Above: Katz's Deli, NYC.

Simple saurkraut

Fermented foods are incredibly good for our digestive and immune systems. Since my friend Tim Anderson introduced to me to Katz's epic book, *The Art of Fermentation*, I've been getting up to all kinds of experiments in my prep kitchen. Kimchi is probably my most favoured, but if I'm looking for something more subtle, sauerkraut is my go-to fermented vegetable. It is easy to make and is a deliciously tangy accompaniment to lots of sandwiches, stews and dumplings.

1 white cabbage
1¼ teaspoons rock salt
1 teaspoon caraway seeds

MAKES 1 LITRE/QUART

Remove the outer leaves of the cabbage. Set aside. Slice the remaining cabbage as thinly as you can with a large, sharp knife. Place in a large bowl and add the salt.

Mix the cabbage and salt well, mixing and squeezing with your hands for 12–15 minutes. Once the cabbage has softened and there is a good amount of liquid in your bowl, add the caraway seeds. Mix well.

Start adding the cabbage and liquid to a sterilized jar. Once half filled, use your hand to squash down the cabbage ensuring that it is well compressed into the jar and covered by the liquid. Fill the rest of the jar, pushing the cabbage down. There should be no gaps or spaces in the jar and the cabbage should be covered by liquid. Ensure there is a small space at the top of the jar. Seal the lid and place out of direct sunlight for 2 weeks. The longer you leave it, the more tangy it will be. Check the taste after 2–3 weeks and, when you are happy with the flavour, transfer it into smaller jars. These will keep for 6 months in the fridge.

FISH ARE MY FRIENDS
Tacos with crispy coconut and cauliflower

I walked (and jogged) down many many LA streets in search of vegan taco trucks. The fish taco is everywhere, but the vegan ones takes a little more searching. But I don't mind the searching. It works off the calories for your five-meals-a-day diet that downtown LA demands; such is the quality of the eating here. There's something very comforting about a crispy hot filling with crunchy 'slaw and tangy sauces, all wrapped up in a soft taco. I guarantee this recipe will win over your most pescatarian of friends.

TO MAKE THE CAULIFLOWER
1 cauliflower, cut into
   3–5-cm/1½–2-inch
   florets

TO MAKE THE BATTER
½ teaspoon salt
45 g/1 cup panko
   breadcrumbs
35 g/¼ cup cornmeal/
   polenta
25 g/⅓ cup coarse
   desiccated/dried
   unsweetened shredded
   coconut
2 teaspoons smoked
   paprika
1 teaspoon ground cumin
½ teaspoon garlic
   powder
¼ teaspoon ground
   turmeric
1 teaspoon fine salt
½ teaspoon ground white
   pepper
240 ml/1 cup coconut
   milk
grated zest and freshly
   squeezed juice of 1 lime

TO MAKE THE TACO 'SLAW
½ small red cabbage,
   finely sliced
¼ white cabbage, finely
   sliced

1 large carrot, peeled
   and grated
1–2 small red chillies/
   chiles, finely chopped,
   to taste
small handful of fresh
   coriander/cilantro,
   roughly chopped
freshly squeezed juice
   of 1 lime
1 tablespoon white
   vinegar
1–2 tablespoons maple
   syrup, to taste
½ teaspoon salt

TO MAKE THE VEGAN
TARTARE SAUCE
3 tablespoons vegan
   mayonnaise
   (see page 12)
2 dill pickles, finely
   chopped
freshly squeezed juice
   of ½ lime
1 tablespoon freshly
   chopped dill
pinch of salt

TO SERVE
8–10 blue corn tortillas
hot sauce (optional)
lime wedges

baking sheet, lightly oiled
baking sheet, lined

SERVES 4–6

Preheat the oven to 210°C (410°F) Gas 6.

Place the florets on the oiled baking sheet and bake in the oven for 15–20 minutes until nicely roasted and starting to brown.

Prepare the 'slaw by adding all the ingredients into a large mixing bowl and mixing well so that all the vegetables are well coated. Set aside for at least 30–40 minutes so that the cabbage will start to soften.

In a bowl, mix together all the dry ingredients for the batter. In another bowl, whisk together the coconut milk, lime zest and juice.

Dip pieces of cauliflower in the coconut mixture, then roll in the panko breadcrumb mixture to coat. Lay the pieces onto the lined baking sheet. Bake in the preheated oven for 20–30 minutes, turning occasionally, until crispy and golden on all sides.

Meanwhile, prepare the vegan tartare sauce by mixing all the ingredients together in a small bowl. Set aside.

Place a small, clean frying pan/skillet over high heat and cook the tacos for 1–2 minutes on each side until softened and warm. Then add a spoonful of 'slaw and top with a couple of pieces of crispy cauliflower. Dress with a little tartare sauce and a dash of hot sauce, if you like. Serve immediately with lime wedges on the side.

CHKN 'N' WAFFLES *Crispy fried seitan 'chicken' with polenta waffles*

If the coastal towns of Maryland and Delaware felt like the all-American holiday destination, then fried chicken and waffles was one of the all-American dishes. This vegan take on crispy deep-fried chicken, like much of the American approach to their vegan food (as well as their confident fusion), makes no apologies for its meaty re-imagination and can be served on its own with hot sauce or however meat-eaters like to eat their fried chicken. You can even make nuggets out of this recipe if you like. You need a waffle iron to make waffles, but you could just make waffle pancakes at a push.

TO MAKE THE 'CHKN'

2 garlic cloves, crushed
120 g/4 oz. organic vital wheat gluten
40 g/scant 1 cup nutritional yeast
2 teaspoons onion powder
½ teaspoon herbamare seasoning
1 teaspoon fresh thyme (or ¼ teaspoon dried)
1 heaped teaspoon fresh marjoram or oregano (or use ½ teaspoon dried)
½ teaspoon mustard powder
½ tablespoon tahini
120 ml/½ cup vegetable stock

TO MAKE THE CRISPY BATTER

250 g/9 oz. puffed rice, such as Rice Krispies
½ teaspoon fine rock salt
½ teaspoon freshly ground black pepper
3–4 tablespoons vegan mayonnaise (see page 12)

TO MAKE THE WAFFLES

480 ml/2 cups almond or other vegan milk
1 teaspoon freshly squeezed lemon juice or apple cider vinegar
180 g/1¼ cups fine cornmeal/polenta
120 g/scant 1 cup plain/all-purpose flour
½ teaspoon salt
2 tablespoons brown sugar
1½ tablespoons baking powder
¼ teaspoon ground cinnamon
2 tablespoons pomace or vegetable oil, plus extra for brushing

TO SERVE

maple syrup
coconut or vegan butter
salt

baking sheet, lightly oiled waffle iron (optional)

SERVES 4

Preheat the oven to 180°C (350°F) Gas 4. Half-fill a deep baking pan with water, add the crushed garlic cloves and place in the oven.

Mix the dry ingredients for the 'chkn' in a bowl and make a well in the centre. In a jug/pitcher, mix together the tahini and stock and pour into the well. Combine to make a stiff dough and knead well (I like to use a machine). Roll out the dough on a floured surface to 2 cm/¾ inch thickness. Slice into goujons, 6 x 2.5 cm/2½ x 1 inch. Place the 'chkn' pieces into the water bath in the oven. Cover with foil and bake for 40 minutes. Remove and drain on paper towels.

Turn up the oven to 190°C (375°F) Gas 5.

Place the puffed rice in a small bowl and scrunch to coarse crumbs. Add the salt and pepper, and mix well. Place the vegan mayonnaise in another bowl. Dip the 'chkn' pieces into the mayo, then dip into the rice to coat. Lay the pieces on the oiled baking sheet and bake for 18–20 minutes until golden and crispy.

Preheat a waffle iron or heavy-bottomed frying pan/skillet. Mix together the almond milk and lemon juice; set aside. In a large bowl, whisk together the cornmeal/polenta, flour, salt, sugar, baking powder and cinnamon. Make a well in the centre and add the milk mixture and oil. Mix well to make a thick batter.

Brush the waffle iron or pan with oil and add the batter. Cook according to the waffle iron instructions (or for 3–5 minutes each side in a pan) until golden. Serve the waffles with maple syrup, a few knobs of butter, some 'chkn' pieces and a sprinkle of salt.

JACK'S WIFE FREDA KNOWS COMFORT
Green shakshuka with minted almond 'ricotta'

Our North American cousins could really teach us a thing or two about brunch. And one of the best places to go for brunch on NYC's Lower East Side is a place called Jack's Wife Freda. People queue for hours for her Green Shakshuka. So I decided we needed a vegan version, that works beautifully without the eggs. The minted 'ricotta' is delicious alongside the smoky spinach and kale. Thick slices of sourdough (see page 75) establish this dish as a solid brunch or lunch with the comfort factor.

TO MAKE THE SHAKSHUKA
1–2 tablespoons olive oil
1 small onion, finely chopped
4 plump garlic cloves, crushed
  and finely chopped
1 large or 2 small leeks, halved
  lengthways, thinly sliced and
  rinsed
1 red chilli/chile, finely chopped
  (deseed if you prefer)
1½ teaspoons ground cumin
2 teaspoons smoked paprika
pinch of dried thyme
100 g/3½ oz. kale, sliced
200 g/7 oz. frozen or fresh spinach
  (or use Swiss chard)
1 green (bell) pepper, cut into
  1-cm/⅜-inch chunks
500 ml/2 cups water
½–1 teaspoon salt, to taste
½ teaspoon freshly ground black
  pepper

TO SERVE
120 ml/½ cup almond 'ricotta'
  with fresh mint (see page 15)
4 thick slices sourdough
  (see page 75)
chilli/chili garlic oil or hot sauce

SERVES 4

Heat the olive oil in a large frying pan/skillet over medium-high heat, add the onion and sauté for 8–10 minutes until softened. Add the garlic and leeks and cook for a further 2–3 minutes. Add the chilli/chile, cumin, paprika and thyme. Stir well and set aside.

Place all of the kale into a food processor with half the spinach, half the chopped green (bell) pepper and the water. Blend to a smooth, thick batter and then pour into the onion and garlic pan. Place over medium heat and add the remaining spinach and pepper. Bring to a simmer and cook for 10–12 minutes. Add a little more liquid if needed and season with salt and pepper, to taste. It should be the consistency of thick porridge/oatmeal.

To serve, pour the mixture into a wide, deep ovenproof dish and then lay 7–8 spoonfuls of the minted almond 'ricotta' on the top, or use your hands if easier. Place the dish under a hot grill/broiler for 4–5 minutes. Serve immediately with thick toasted slices of sourdough and a drizzle of chilli/chili garlic oil or hot sauce if you like.

JUST PEACHY
cobbler pots

This southern comfort pudding is an old-fashioned classic, and I'm reluctant to stray too far from the original because it's incredibly delicious and can easily be made from simple store cupboard ingredients. Peaches are my daughter's favourite, so we sampled a few peach cobblers along the southern routes, for research purposes of course. You can make this dessert in a single dish if you prefer and it's incredibly quick to assemble.

190 g/6½ oz. vegan margarine
120 g/scant 1 cup self-raising/
    self-rising flour
180 g/scant 1 cup brown sugar,
    plus ½ tablespoon to sprinkle
½ teaspoon fine salt
100 ml/scant ½ cup vegan milk
2 400-g/14-oz. cans sliced peaches
    in juice, drained
1½ teaspoons ground cinnamon,
    plus ½ teaspoon to sprinkle
¼ teaspoon freshly grated nutmeg
½ tablespoon cornflour/cornstarch

*1 ovenproof dish or 6 individual
   ramekins*

SERVES 6

Preheat the oven to 180°C (350°F) Gas 4.

Melt the vegan margarine. You can do this by placing it straight into the ovenproof dish (or equally dividing it between the individual ramekins), and placing them on a baking sheet in the warming oven.

Mix together the flour, sugar and cinnamon, then blend together with the milk to make a batter. Pour the batter into the baking dish or divide it between the individual ramekins. Do not stir. Carefully place the drained peach pieces into the batter, where they will sink a little. Be careful not to move them around or mix the batter at all.

Add an extra sprinkle of cinnamon and brown sugar across the top of each pot, or dish. Bake in the preheated oven until golden on top and set in the middle; 30–40 minutes for individual pots and 50–55 minutes for one large dish. Serve immediately.

PECAN CRUMBLE COOKIE *and blueberry*
ice—cream sammie

My early food experiences in America mostly involved nursing a broken heart over various giant tubs of ice-cream on the Lower East Side of Manhattan as a naïve 19-year-old. It was also my first introduction to proper brunching and frozen margaritas (and that you can't run away from a broken heart). I gained 7 kg/15 lb. within a month or two and soon realised that having aisles of cookies and ice-cream available to me did not mean I had to eat all the cookies and ice-cream available to me. You can simply enjoy the soft cookies on their own, but they make a fun dessert that can be prepared in advance. It is better to make them smaller (and eat two!) so they don't melt too quickly.

TO MAKE THE COOKIES

- 180 g/generous 1½ cups pecans, roughly chopped
- 320 g/2½ cups plain/all-purpose flour
- 1 teaspoon bicarbonate of soda/baking soda
- 1 teaspoon ground cinnamon
- ½ teaspoon salt
- 1 teaspoon cornflour/cornstarch
- 160 g/5½ oz. coconut oil or vegan butter
- 150 g/¾ cup soft brown sugar
- 2 flax 'eggs' (see page 15) or egg replacer
- ½ vanilla pod/bean, seeds scraped (or use ¼ teaspoon vanilla paste)
- 60 g/2¼ oz. vegan suet

TO MAKE THE FILLING

- 450 g/1 lb. Ginger's vanilla malt ice-cream with blueberry ripple (see page 58)

2 baking sheets, lined

SERVES 6

Preheat the oven to 170°C (340°F) Gas 4.

Place the chopped pecans on a baking sheet and put in the oven for approx. 15 minutes until lightly toasted. Set aside.

In a medium bowl, mix together the flour, bicarbonate of soda/baking soda, cinnamon, salt and cornflour/cornstarch. Then in a large mixing bowl, beat together the coconut oil or vegan butter with the sugar until it's fluffy, light and creamy. Carefully beat in the flax 'eggs' and vanilla, and then add the flour mixture, to make a fairly stiff dough. Add the toasted pecans and suet and mix well.

Wrap the dough in clingfilm/plastic wrap and chill in the fridge for several hours, or overnight is preferable. The longer the chilling, the better the cookie crumbles.

Remove the dough from the fridge and let sit at room temperature for 20–30 minutes. Preheat the oven to 180°C (350°F) Gas 4.

Break off chunks of cookie dough and roll into balls, according to the size you prefer. Make 12 balls for large cookies or 20 or so for smaller cookies. Lay on the lined baking sheets leaving plenty of space between the dough balls.

Bake the cookies in the preheated oven for 10–12 minutes, rotating the sheets halfway through, until the cookies are slightly golden brown around the edges. Remove from the oven and allow to cool for 5 minutes on the baking sheets. The cookies will deflate slightly as they cool. If they look too puffy, flatten them gently with the back of a spoon. Transfer the cookies to a wire rack to cool.

When ready to serve, remove the blueberry rippled ice-cream from the freezer and allow to soften slightly for 10–15 minutes. Place a small scoop of ice-cream on a cookie. Spread slightly to ensure it almost reaches the edges. Top the ice-cream with another cookie, and, using your palm, gently press down to create a sandwich. Serve immediately.

AIN'T NO VOODOO *raspberry chai doughnut*

During my last trip to the US, I think I spent at least an entire day lining up for good food in total. Most of the time it was worth it. Sometimes it was even worth getting in line again, in a different city. Of all the lines I waited in across the US, the longest one of all was outside Voodoo Doughnut in Portland, Oregon. Fortunately the queue in their Austin branch in Texas was much shorter. I'm sure it was the offer of one of our doughnuts (and apologies for tourist stupidity) which encouraged the local constabulary to let us off with a warning for our dubious parking that night. The range of doughnuts, with many, many vegan options, is simply off the scale in Voodoo. It has to be seen to be believed. My favourites were the Portland Cream and the insanely large Apple Fritter (see adaptation right). But it was when I was playing around with some new flavours at home that I made a chai sugar version. I think the folks at Voodoo would be suitably impressed.

TO MAKE THE DOUGH

240 ml/1 cup unsweetened
    soy milk
50 g/¼ cup coconut sugar
    or unrefined brown sugar
14 g/½ oz. fast-action dried yeast
280 g/2 cups strong bread flour,
    plus extra for dusting
¼ teaspoon fine salt
½ teaspoon baking powder
1–2 pinches of freshly grated
    nutmeg
¼ teaspoon ground cinnamon
60 g/2¼ oz. vegan suet

TO MAKE THE SPICED SUGAR

80 g/scant ½ cup coconut sugar
2 teaspoons chai spice mix
    (see page 156)

TO FILL AND FRY THE DOUGHNUTS

1 small jar of high-quality raspberry
    jam/jelly, such as St Dalfour
about 400 ml/scant 1¾ cups
    pomace or sunflower oil, for
    frying

*5-cm/2-inch round cookie cutter
small piping/pastry bag fitted with
    a round nozzle/tip*

MAKES 8–10

Prepare the spiced sugar at least a day or two earlier, although up to a week would be better. Place the coconut sugar in a small bowl or resealable tub and stir in the freshly ground chai spice mix. Mix well, cover the bowl with clingfilm/plastic wrap or seal the tub with a lid and set aside for a few days or a week if you can.

For the dough, warm the soy milk in a large pan over low heat. Put a few tablespoons of the milk in a small bowl with 1 teaspoon of the sugar. Mix well, then add the yeast. Set aside for 10–15 minutes until frothy.

In a large mixing bowl, whisk the flour, remaining coconut sugar, salt, baking powder, nutmeg, cinnamon and suet. Make a well in the centre and pour in the warm milk and yeast mixture. Knead well for a minute or two and then place in a covered bowl for 1–2 hours until the dough has doubled in size.

Lightly dust the work surface and a couple of baking sheets with flour, then roll out the dough to approx. 2 cm/¾ inch thickness. Using the round cookie cutter, cut out circles of dough and then transfer to the baking sheets. Cover lightly with clingfilm/plastic wrap and leave to rise for another 30–50 minutes.

Pour the oil for frying into a large wok or deep pan to about 5 cm/ 2 inches deep. Heat the oil over medium-high heat to 180°C/350°F, until a pinch of dough gently sizzles and rises to top.

Fry the doughnuts, in batches to ensure the pan isn't crowded, for 2–3 minutes on each side until golden brown, but not too dark. Drain on paper towels.

Sift the chai sugar into a large bowl to ensure any big pieces of spice are removed. Place the warm doughnuts into the sugar and toss until well coated. Set aside on a tray to cool further.

Once the doughnuts are cooled, fill a small piping/pastry bag with raspberry jam/jelly, make a small hole in the side of the doughnuts using a skewer or small spoon, then insert the nozzle/tip into the doughnut. Fill each doughnut with jam/jelly, being careful not to overfill and burst the doughnut. These doughnuts are best enjoyed within 24 hours.

Alternatively, you can simply glaze your doughnuts with flavoured icing/frosting or make an apple fritter. To make an apple fritter, simply cover half the rolled-out dough with fruit, then fold over the other half and press down gently. Slice the dough into random small squares, place on a baking sheet and cover with clingfilm/plastic wrap. Leave to rise somewhere warm for 1–2 hours until the dough has doubled in size, then fry as above. Fritters are great simply drizzled with a vanilla glaze.

INDEX

A

aduki beans: dirty beans 185–7
almonds: almond milk 12
  almond 'ricotta'/cream 15
  minted 'ricotta' 15
  pear and frangipane tart 96
arepa biscuits 178
artichokes: artichoke torta 88
  BBQ artichokes 166
asparagus: campfire risotto 76
aubergines/eggplants:
  baked aubergine fries 80
  Big Ass bagnat 72
  Bombay Frankie masala vegetable roti wrap 128
  roasted aubergine lasagne 91
avocados: creamy dreamy quesadilla 181
  Tevo's Texan scramble breakfast burrito 177

B

'bacon': tempeh 'bacon', lettuce and tomato sandwich 25
bagnat, Big Ass 72
Bake O'Rama's chocolate cake 52–3
banana, Cambodian-style fried 152
banana flower, crispy 140
bara 162
basil oil 22
BBQ artichokes 166
BBQ rub, 'magic dust' 184
BBQ sauce 80
  Louisiana-style 184
bean curd sticks: crispy jerk skins 38
bean sprouts: Singaporean laksa 138–9
beans: black bean salsa 178
  dirty beans 185–7
  homemade beans 26
  Ital stew 37
  lime and ginger-glazed

black beans 143
'bechamel' sauce 91
beetroot/beets: baked beetroot and horseradish mornay 41
  beetroot and watercress samosas 111–13
  beetroot pakoda kadhi 119–21
  big beet burger 170–3
  Bombay vegetable sandwich 114
  the Reuben, honestly 188–91
bhaji, pav 108–9
Big Ass bagnat 72
big beet burger 170–3
biscuits see cookies
black beans: black bean salsa 178
  lime and ginger-glazed black beans 143
Blasket bunny 34–6
Bombay Frankie masala vegetable roti wrap 128
Bombay vegetable sandwich 114
Bordelaise suet pudding 79
bread: bara 162
  Bombay Frankie masala vegetable roti wrap 128
  cashew cheese croutons 64
  crusty soda bread 34–6
  easy fluffy naan 124
  pain de campagne 75
  pea and methi stuffed parathas 127
  quinoa bread 190–1
  turmeric rolls 108–9
  see also sandwiches
burger, big beet 170–3
burger sauce 173
Burmese-style hot sauce 136
burrito, Tevo's Texan scramble breakfast 177
bus station rice 132–3
butter masala gravy 164-5
buttercream, chocolate 53

C

cabbage: Savoy-wrapped quinoa roast 42
  simple sauerkraut 191
  slaw 128, 192
Cajun spice powder 182
cakes: Bake O'Rama's chocolate cake 52–3
  pineapple and cardamom upside-down cake 155
'calamari' rings 138–9
Cambodian-style fried banana 152
Cambodian-style pickled vegetables 135
Cambodian yellow curry 140
campfire risotto 76
candied kumquats 98–9
caper bites, crispy 46
cashew nuts: cashew cheese croutons 64
  cashew cheese sauce 174
  cashew cream 12
  cauliflower mac 'n' jack 46
  Savoy-wrapped quinoa roast 42
cauliflower: cauliflower mac 'n' jack 46
  cauliflower 'steak' with green peppercorn sauce 29
  crispy coconut and lime cauliflower 192
  Korean-style cauliflower wings 168–9
chai-spiced rice pudding 156
channa dal: marinara vegball sub 174
  no shimi shami kebab 123
'cheese': baked beetroot and horseradish mornay 41
  cashew cheese sauce 174
  marinara vegball sub 174
  Punjabi poutine 164–5
  the Reuben, honestly 188–91
  roasted aubergine lasagne 91
  vegan substitutes 10
  see also 'ricotta'
'chicken', crispy fried seitan 195

chickpea/garbanzo bean flour: panisse 71
  beetroot pakoda kadhi 119–21
chickpeas/garbanzo beans: chickpea curry 162
  macadamia crumble pots 30
  Moroccan-style vegetable claypot 92
  sofrito-style Mediterranean stew 87
chillies/chiles: Burmese-style hot sauce 136
  chilli pickle 17
  Dougie's hot habanero sauce 38
  red curry paste 131
  salted chilli olive oil 95
Chinese leaves: Nanban's vegan ramen 144
chkn n waffles 195
chocolate cake, Bake O'Rama's 52–3
chowder, sweetcorn 178
chutney: 'green' chutney 114
  quick pineapple chutney 113
cilantro see coriander
cobbler pots, just peachy 199
coconut: tacos with crispy coconut and cauliflower 192
  Korean-style cauliflower wings 168–9
coconut milk: chai-spiced rice pudding 156
  Singaporean laksa 138–9
cookies: arepa biscuits 178
  ginger cookies 156
  pecan crumble cookie and blueberry ice-cream sarnie 200
coriander/cilantro: 'green' chutney 114
cornmeal/polenta: arepa biscuits 178
  polenta waffles 195
cottage pie, my big fat veggie 45
courgette flower, tempura 67
'crab cakes' 131
croquetas, shiitake mushroom 84

croquettes, Khmer 135
croutons, cashew cheese 64
crumbles: macadamia
    crumble pots 30
    plum and pistachio
        crumble 54
curry: Cambodian yellow
    curry 140
    chickpea curry 162
    Khmer croquettes 135
    red curry paste 131
    Singaporean laksa 138–9
custard 54

D
Dad's dinner 67
daikon/mooli, braised 144
dairy products, vegan
    substitutes 10
dashi, mushroom 144
demi-glace 79
Dijon pie 32–3
dill pickles 173
dirty beans 185–7
doughnut, raspberry chai
    202–3
Dougie's hot habanero
    sauce 38
dressings see sauces
dumplings: beetroot
    pakoda kadhi 119–21
    cumin-spiced johnny
        cakes 37
    loaded pierogi 49
    miso dauphinoise
        dumplings 143
    sofrito-style
        Mediterranean stew 87

E
eggplants see aubergines
eggs: flax 'egg' 15

F
Filipino breakfast rice 147
flaxseeds: flax 'egg' 15
frangipane: pear and
    frangipane tart 96
French onion soup 64
fries, masala 164–5
fritters: 'calamari' rings
    138–9
    Cambodian-style fried
        banana 152
    crispy banana flower 140

crispy okra 185–7
Khmer croquettes 135
Korean-style cauliflower
    wings 168–9
lotus root 136
panisse 71
pickles 173
raspberry chai doughnut
    202–3
shiitake mushroom
    croquetas 84
tempura courgette
    flowers 67

G
ganache 53
garbanzo beans see
    chickpeas
ginger: ginger cookies 156
    lime and ginger-glazed
        black beans 143
    Ginger's vanilla malt ice-
        cream 58
gravy: butter masala gravy
    164–5
    miso gravy 17
'green' chutney 114
green shakshuka 196
Guinness: vegetable and
    Guinness stew 34–6
gungo beans: Ital stew 37

H
habanero sauce 38
haricot/navy beans:
    homemade beans 26
harissa-roasted vegetables
    83
hoisin sauce 151
horseradish: baked
    beetroot and
    horseradish mornay 41

I
ice-cream: Ginger's vanilla
    malt ice-cream 58
    pecan crumble cookie
        and blueberry ice-cream
        sarnie 200
Ital stew 37

J
jackfruit: po-boy with
    NOLA-style jackfruit 182
Jack's Wife Freda 196

jayk chien 152
jerk skins, crispy 38
Jerusalem artichokes
    with garlic cream and
    hazelnut crust 50
johnny cakes, cumin-spiced
    37

K
kachori chaat, spinach and
    nasturtium 117–18
kadhi, beetroot pakoda
    119–21
ketchup: BBQ sauce 80
    burger sauce 173
    Louisiana-style BBQ sauce
        184
Khmer croquettes 135
Korean-style cauliflower
    wings 168–9
kumquats, candied 98–9

L
laksa, Singaporean 138–9
lasagne, roasted aubergine
    91
leeks: green shakshuka 196
lentils: my big fat veggie
    cottage pie 45
    Punjabi pie and gravy
        104–7
    roasted aubergine lasagne
        with Puy lentils 91
lime: lime and ginger-glazed
    black beans 143
loaded pierogi 49
lotus root: Cambodian
    yellow curry 140
    lotus root with Burmese-
        style hot sauce 136
Louisiana-style BBQ sauce
    184

M
macadamia nuts: macadamia
    crumble pots 30
    ranch-style dressing 166
macaroni: cauliflower mac
    'n' jack 46
'magic dust' BBQ rub 184
malt powder: Ginger's
    vanilla malt ice-cream 58
mango coulis 156
marinara vegball sub 174
masala fries 164–5

mayonnaise: burger sauce
    173
    easy vegan mayonnaise 12
    remoulade 182
    saffron mayonnaise 88
    vegan tartare sauce 192
Mediterranean stew 87
methi leaves: pea and methi
    stuffed parathas 127
milk: almond milk 12
mince (vegan): marinara
    vegball sub 174
    my big fat veggie cottage
        pie 45
    no shimi shami kebab 123
minted 'ricotta' 15, 196
miso paste: miso dauphinoise
    dumplings 143
    miso gravy 17
Mississippi mash 185–7
mock duck pancakes 151
mooli see daikon
Moroccan-style vegetable
    claypot 92
mushrooms: Bordelaise
    suet pudding 79
    loaded pierogi 49
    mushroom dashi 144
    Savoy-wrapped quinoa
        roast 42
    shiitake mushroom
        croquetas 84
    vegetable and Guinness
        stew 34–6
my big fat veggie cottage
    pie 45

N
naan, easy fluffy 124
Nanban's vegan ramen 144
nasturtium leaves: spinach
    and nasturtium kachori
    chaat 117–18
navy beans see haricot beans
noodles: Cambodian yellow
    curry 140
    Nanban's vegan ramen 144
    Sichuan hot and sour
        sweet potato noodles
        148–9
    Singaporean laksa 138–9
nori dressing 144
num banh chok 140
nutritional yeast see yeast,
    nutritional

O

oats: macadamia crumble pots 30
  plum and pistachio crumble 54
okra, crispy 185–7
olive oil: basil oil 22
  olive oil mash 33
  salted chilli olive oil 95
olives: tapenade 72
onion soup, French 64

P

paella with harissa-roasted vegetables 83
pain de campagne 75
palm hearts: 'calamari' rings 138–9
  Thai-style redcakes 131
pancakes, crispy mock duck 151
panisse 71
panna cotta 98–9
paprika: paprika tortilla straws 22
parathas, pea and methi stuffed 127
passionfruit syrup 152
pasta: cauliflower mac 'n' jack 46
  roasted aubergine lasagne 91
pastry: suet pastry 79
  vegan pastry 16
pav bhaji 108–9
peaches: just peachy cobbler pots 199
pear and frangipane tart 96
peas: Khmer croquettes 135
  pea and methi stuffed parathas 127
  see also split peas
pecan crumble cookie and blueberry ice-cream sarnie 200
peppercorns: green peppercorn sauce 29
peppers: Big Ass bagnat 72
  green shakshuka 196
  remoulade 182
pickles 173
  Cambodian-style pickled vegetables 135
  chilli pickle 17
pierogi, loaded 49

pies: artichoke torta 88
  deep Dijon pie 32–3
  Punjabi pie and gravy 104–7
pineapple: pineapple and cardamom upside-down cake 155
  quick pineapple chutney 113
pinto beans: dirty beans 185–7
pistachio nuts: plum and pistachio crumble 54
pizza, socca 68
plum and pistachio crumble 54
po-boy with NOLA-style jackfruit 182
polenta see cornmeal
potatoes: Khmer croquettes 135
  masala fries 164–5
  miso dauphinoise dumplings 143
  Mississippi mash 185–7
  my big fat veggie cottage pie 45
  olive oil mash 33
  Punjabi pie and gravy 104–7
  root veg rosti 26
  sweetcorn chowder 178
  Tevo's Texan scramble breakfast burrito 177
  Thai-style redcakes 131
poutine, Punjabi 164–5
puffed rice: crispy fried seitan 'chicken' 195
Punjabi pie and gravy 104–7
Punjabi poutine 164–5

Q

quesadilla, creamy dreamy 181
quinoa: Moroccan-style vegetable claypot 92
  quinoa bread 190–1
  Savoy-wrapped quinoa roast 42

R

ramen, Nanban's vegan 144
ranch-style dressing 166
raspberry chai doughnut 202–3

red cabbage: taco slaw 192
red curry paste 131
redcakes, Thai-style 131
remoulade 182
the Reuben, honestly 188–91
rhubarb: sticky toffee and rhubarb pudding 57
rice: artichoke torta 88
  bus station rice 132–3
  campfire risotto 76
  chai-spiced rice pudding 156
  Filipino breakfast rice 147
  paella 83
'ricotta': almond 'ricotta'/cream 15
  minted 'ricotta' 15, 196
risotto, campfire 76
rosti, root veg 26
roti wraps, Bombay Frankie masala vegetable 128

S

saffron mayonnaise 88
salsa 181
  black bean salsa 178
salt, truffled 71
samosas, beetroot and watercress 111–13
sandwiches: Big Ass bagnat 72
  Bombay vegetable sandwich 114
  marinara vegball sub 174
  po-boy with NOLA-style jackfruit 182
  the Reuben, honestly 188–91
  tempeh 'bacon', lettuce and tomato sandwich 25
sauces: BBQ sauce 80
  'bechamel' sauce 91
  burger sauce 173
  Burmese-style hot sauce 136
  butter masala gravy 164–5
  cashew cheese sauce 174
  custard 54
  demi-glace 79
  Dougie's hot habanero sauce 38
  green peppercorn sauce 29
  hoisin sauce 151
  kadhi sauce 119–21

Korean-style wing sauce 168–9
  Louisiana-style BBQ sauce 184
  marinara sauce 174
  miso gravy 17
  ranch-style dressing 166
  tamarind sauce 162
  vegan tartare sauce 192
sauerkraut: loaded pierogi 49
  the Reuben, honestly 188–91
  simple sauerkraut 191
Savoy-wrapped quinoa roast 42
seitan 'chicken' 195
shakshuka, green 196
shami kebab, no shimi 123
shiitake mushroom croquetas 84
shio koji tofu 144
Sichuan hot and sour sweet potato noodles 148–9
Singaporean laksa 138–9
sinigag 147
'slaw 128, 192
socca pizza 68
soda bread 34–6
sofrito-style Mediterranean stew 87
soups: French onion soup 64
  Nanban's vegan ramen 144
  roasted tomato soup 22
  Sichuan hot and sour sweet potato noodles 148–9
  sweetcorn chowder 178
spice mixes: Cajun spice powder 182
  chai spice 156
  pav bhaji powder 108–9
spinach: green shakshuka 196
  macadamia crumble pots 30
  socca pizza 68
  spinach and nasturtium kachori chaat 117–18
split peas: big beet burger 170–3
  marinara vegball sub 174
  no shimi shami kebab 123
squash: Cambodian yellow curry 140

macadamia crumble pots 30
stews: Ital stew 37
  sofrito-style Mediterranean stew 87
  vegetable and Guinness stew 34–6
sticky toffee and rhubarb pudding 57
stock, roasted vegetable 16
suan la fen 148–9
suet (vegan): Bordelaise suet pudding 79
  raspberry chai doughnut 202–3
sweet potato noodles, Sichuan hot and sour 148–9
sweetcorn: creamy dreamy quesadilla 181
  sweetcorn chowder 178
  sweetcorn cobs with salted chilli olive oil 95

T
taco 'slaw 192
tacos with crispy coconut and cauliflower 192
tamarind sauce 162
tapenade 72
tartare sauce, vegan 192
tart, pear and frangipane 96
tempeh 26
  the Reuben, honestly 188–91
  tempeh 'bacon', lettuce and tomato sandwich 25
tempura courgette flowers 67
Tevo's Texan scramble breakfast burrito 177
Thai-style redcakes 131
Thai-style vegetable rice 132–3
Tofino Trini double 162
tofu: Savoy-wrapped quinoa roast 42
  shio koji 144
  Singaporean laksa 138–9
  Tevo's Texan scramble breakfast burrito 177
  vegan pastry 16
tomatoes: homemade beans 26
  marinara sauce 174

roasted tomato soup 22
salsa 181
tempeh 'bacon', lettuce and tomato sandwich 25
see also ketchup
tortillas: creamy dreamy quesadilla 181
  paprika tortilla straws 22
  tacos with crispy coconut and cauliflower 192
  Tevo's Texan scramble breakfast burrito 177
turmeric rolls 108–9

V
vegball sub 174
vegetables: Bombay vegetable sandwich 114
  bus station rice 132–3
  Cambodian-style pickled vegetables 135
  harissa-roasted vegetables 83
  Ital stew 37
  Moroccan-style vegetable claypot 92
  my big fat veggie cottage pie 45
  pav bhaji 108–9
  roasted vegetable stock 16
  sofrito-style Mediterranean stew 87
  vegetable and Guinness stew 34–6

W
waffles, polenta 195
watercress: beetroot and watercress samosas 111–13
wraps: Bombay Frankie masala vegetable roti wrap 128
  Tevo's Texan scramble breakfast burrito 177

Y
yeast, nutritional: big beet burger 170–3
  cashew cheese sauce 174
  cauliflower mac 'n' jack 46
  crispy fried seitan 'chicken' 195
  marinara vegball sub 174
yogurt, vegan substitutes 10

PICTURE CREDITS

All travel photographs by Lee James apart from:

Key: a = above; b = below; l = left; c = centre; r = right.

7 cl EyeOn/UIG via Getty Images; 7 ar Dan Herrick/ Getty Images; 20 l Mike Theiss/Getty Images; 20 c raspu/ Getty Images; 20 r Alberto Manuel Urosa Toledano/Getty Images; 21 l Christopher Furlong/Getty Images; 21 ar RA Kearton/Getty Images; 21 br Photofusion/UIG via Getty Images; 34 jbachman56 /istockphoto; 62 l Gerard Julien/AFP/Getty Images; 62 r Dan Herrick/Getty Images; 63 r gianliguori/Getty Images; 71 Fraser Hall/Getty Images; 102 l Punit Paranjpe/AFP/Getty Images; 102 c Sajjad Hussain/AFP/Getty Images; 103 l Cultura RM Exclusive/ Matt Dutile/Getty Images; 103 ar Meinzahn/Getty Images; 103 br Pravut/Getty Images; 111 Saurabh Raj Sharan/Getty Images; 118 Narayan Maharjan/Pacific Press/LightRocket via Getty Images; 124 Clare S Rich/Getty Images; 160 c Kylie McLaughlin/Getty Images; 160 r Heather Binns/ Getty Images; 161 r EddieHernandezPhotography/Getty Images; 185 Camerique/ClassicStock/Getty Images; 191 zazdravnaya/Getty Images.

SUPPLIERS

Here are a few of the online suppliers I use for specialist or unusual produce (such as vital wheat gluten, nutritional yeast, blue corn tortillas and vegan 'charcuterie'):

• For specialist flours, raw and organic ingredients; online supplier with stores in Edinburgh www.realfoods.co.uk
• UK small producer of vegan meats, winner of PETA 2016 Best New Product www.sgaiafoods.co.uk
• Asian produce online www.theasiancookshop.co.uk
• Mexican produce online www.mexgrocer.co.uk
• Specialist produce and online cookstore in the UK www.souschef.co.uk

ACKNOWLEDGEMENTS

I'm forever indebted to my family for supporting me in all my adventures, in food and travels, whether solo or trotting the globe together. Lee, you are my rock upon which I can build my dreams and schemes. And to my children, Roisin and Tevo, thank you for being such compassionate, intelligent and open-minded humans. I hope your adventurousness in the world continues for a very long time. Thanks to my mum, for always being there with words of comfort and encouragement, especially when things have been tough. To my dad for providing me with opportunities to build my own adventures in the world, and my step-mum for our shared foodie fun.

I want to thank everyone at RPS, and the incredible team that works so hard to produce such beautiful books. First and foremost, Clare Winfield and Emily Kydd, whose creative endeavours continue to astound me. My patient and brilliantly precise editor Kate Reeves-Brown; Megan Smith, my wonderful art director; and Tony Hutchinson for his boundless artistic vision. Thank you Cindy Richards and Julia Charles for the opportunity to do all this again, and giving me the flexibility to evolve my work alongside my journeys. Big thanks to the rest of the RPS team, Leslie Harrington and Mai-Ling Collyer.

My foodie journey has led to me to some incredible friendships and colleagues. Huge thanks to my agent, Holly Arnold, for believing in me and guiding me to calmer waters. Big shout out to my street food squad, so many of you to name but you know I love you all! Special big love to Claire Kelsey and Charlotte O'Toole. And to Seema Gupta, thank you for being my fellow greedy girl and helping me see everything more clearly. Thanks to Maya Tincombe for making Vancouver feel like home and introducing me to the spectacular British Colombia. Thanks also to Tim Anderson, for sharing so much learning with me, and to all my MasterChef family and the team at Shine who continue to support me in my endeavours. To David Fox, for giving me the opportunity to flex my creativity at Tampopo restaurants and work with such great kitchen teams.

Massive thanks are also due to all my friends and colleagues who've supported me on my journey especially Zamira Pereira, Michael Caines and John Torode. Also Parin Subba Limbu and Biz Gurung for making Kathmandu a home from home, Becky Elliott and Stephanie Moore, especially for their work with Reach Out to the Community, supporting the most vulnerable people in my hometown of Chorlton. Finally, in memory of our beloved guide and friend Bhattarai Kumar Mahesh, our Sherpa Pasang and cosmic wanderer James Raphael. May Nepal hold you forever in her heart.